For the most curious child I know! I dedicate this little book full of animals to color to you! Have a good time!

T.B.S.P

write your name here

_____

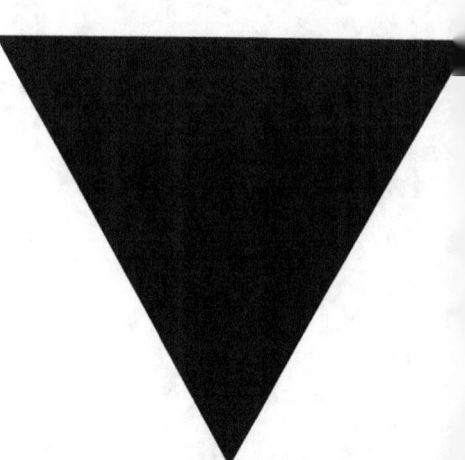

COLOR TESTING

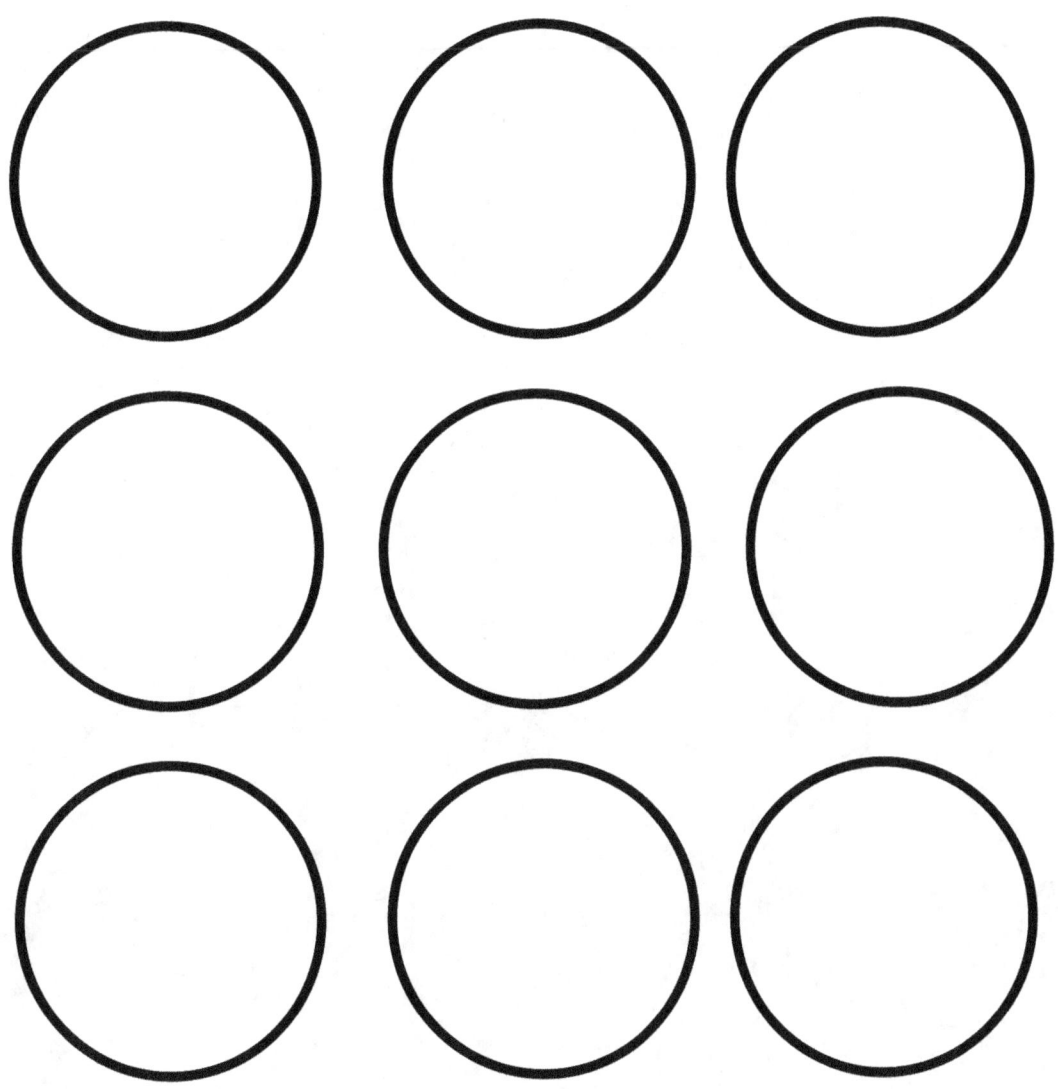

T.B.P.
TAMILLE BARBOSA PUBLICATIONS

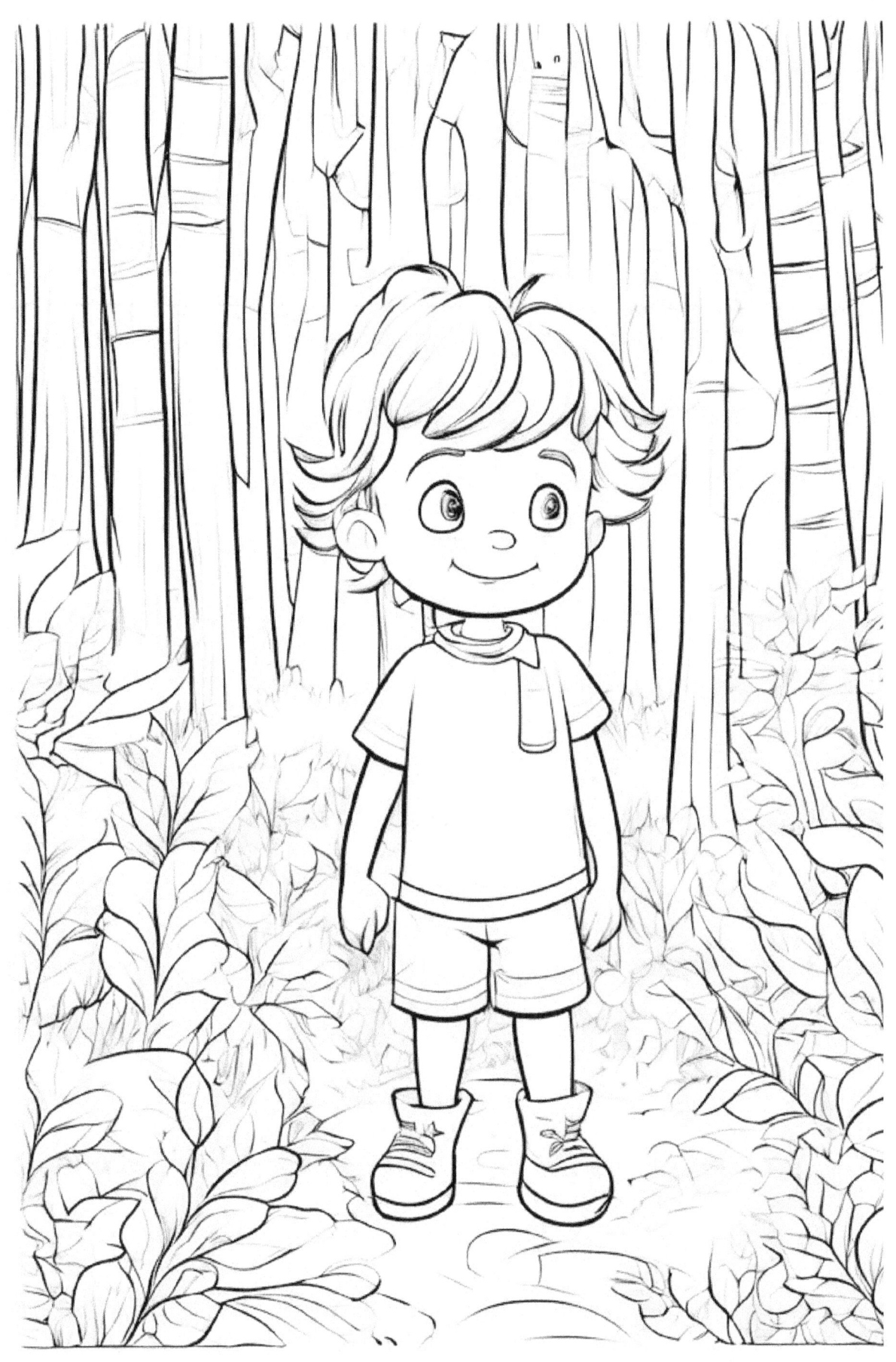

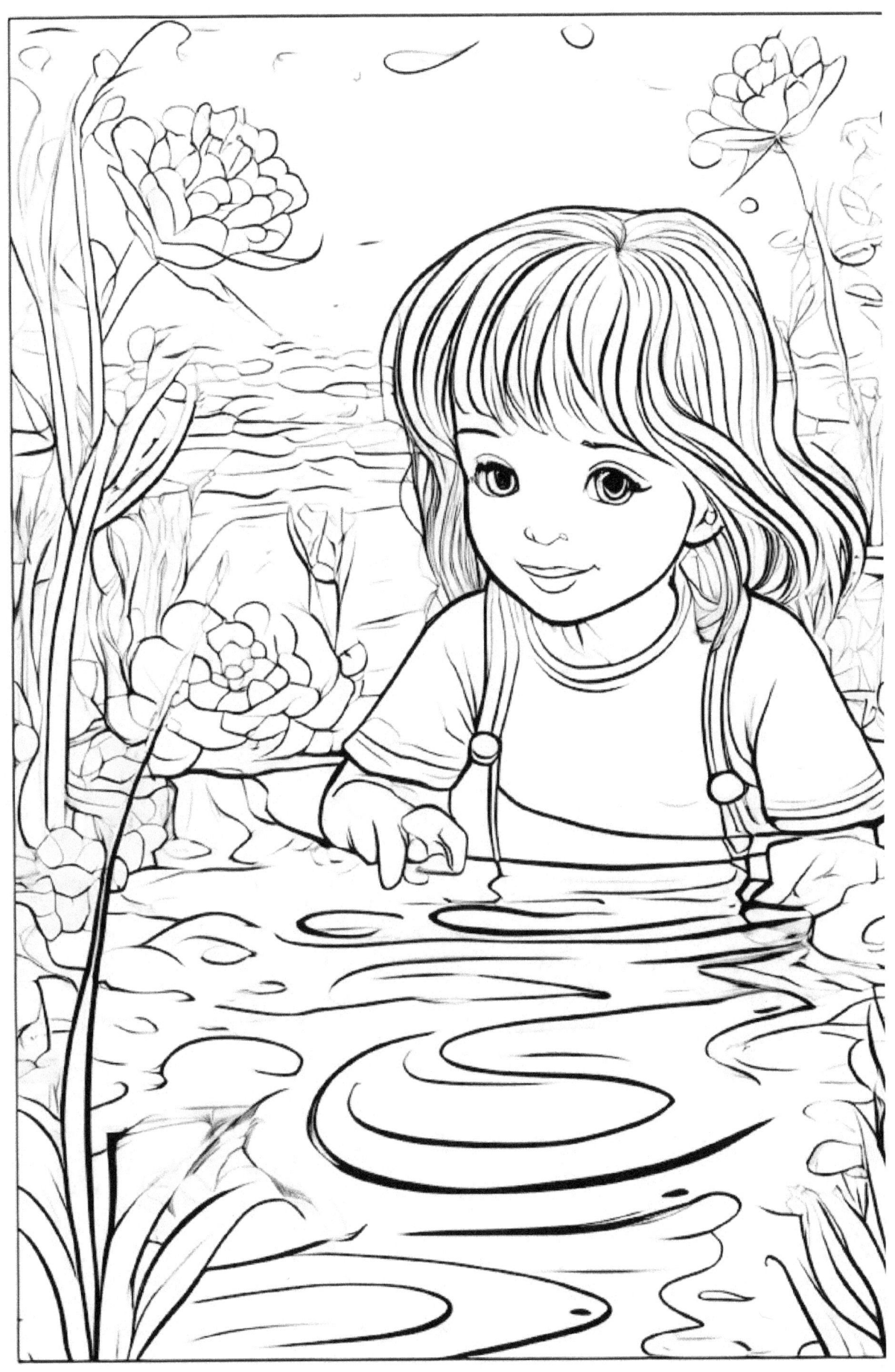

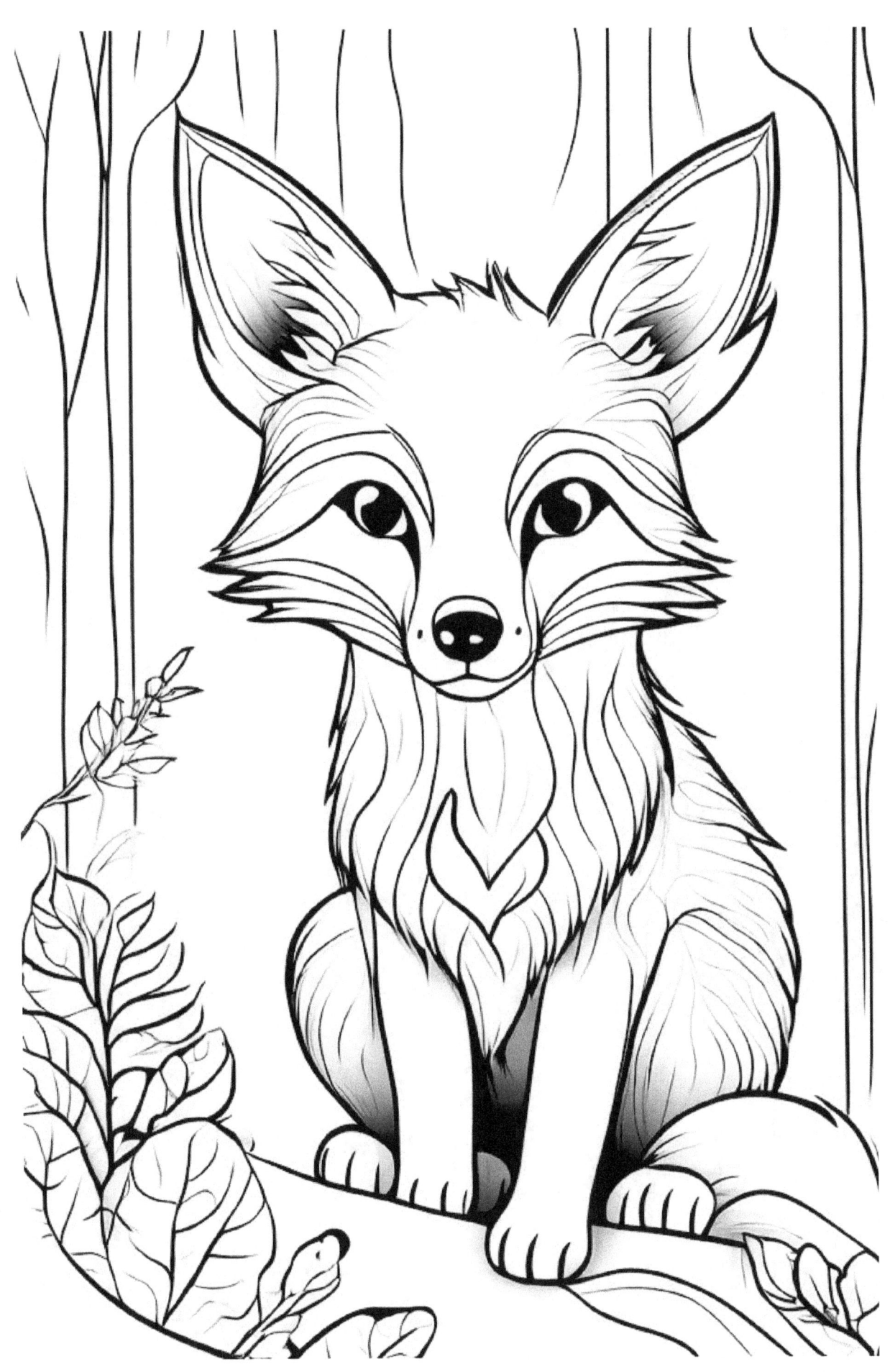

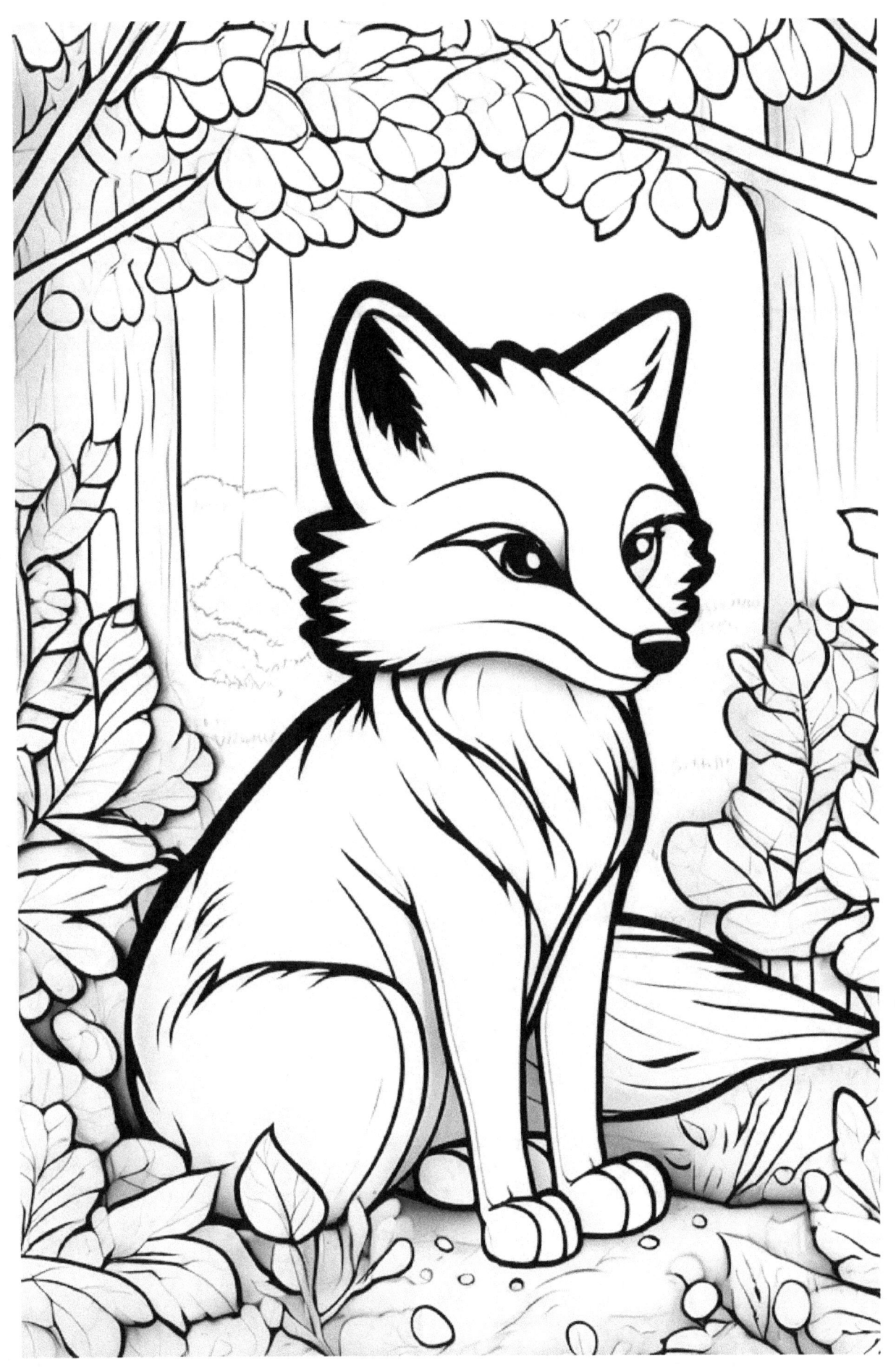

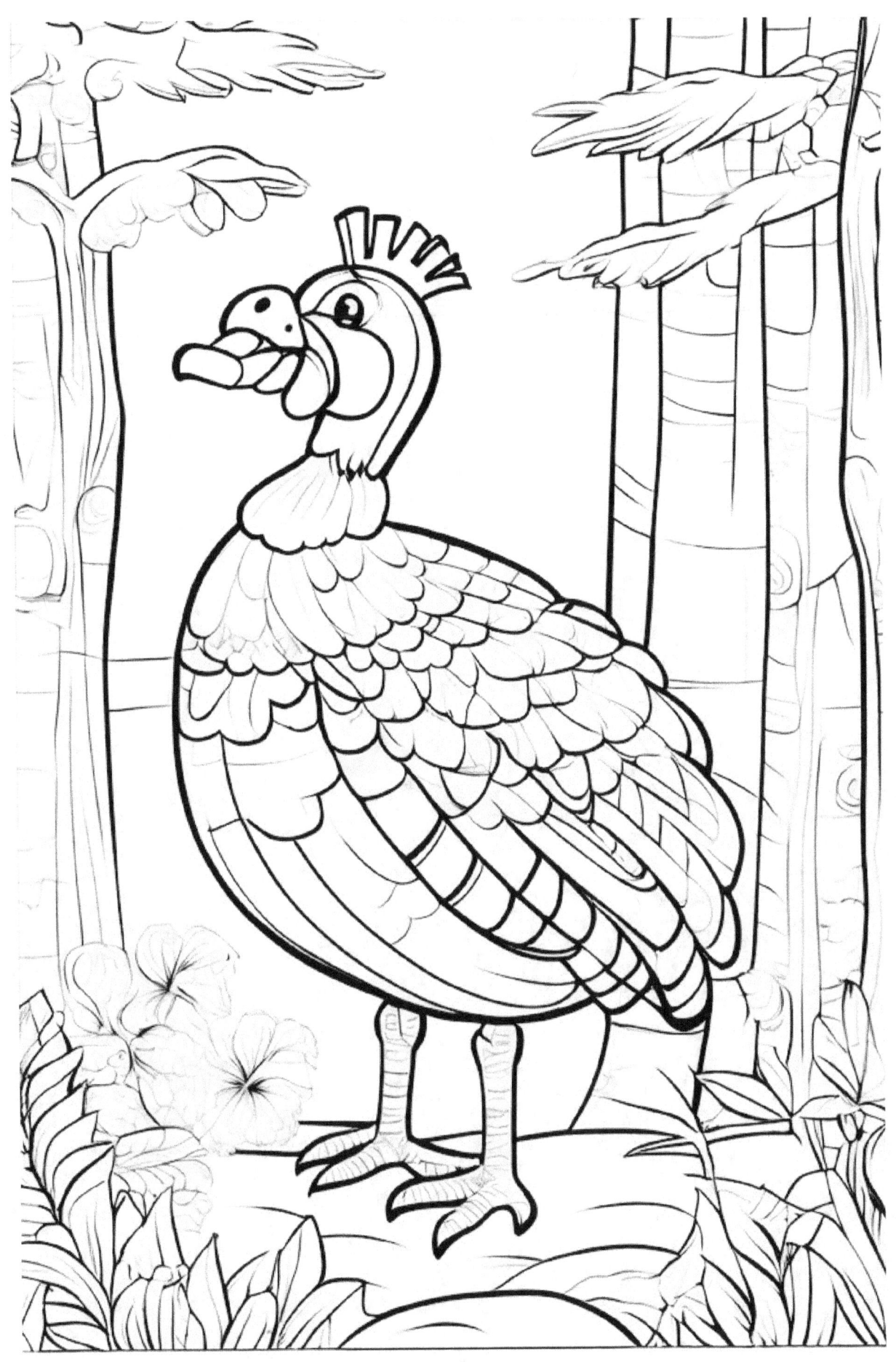

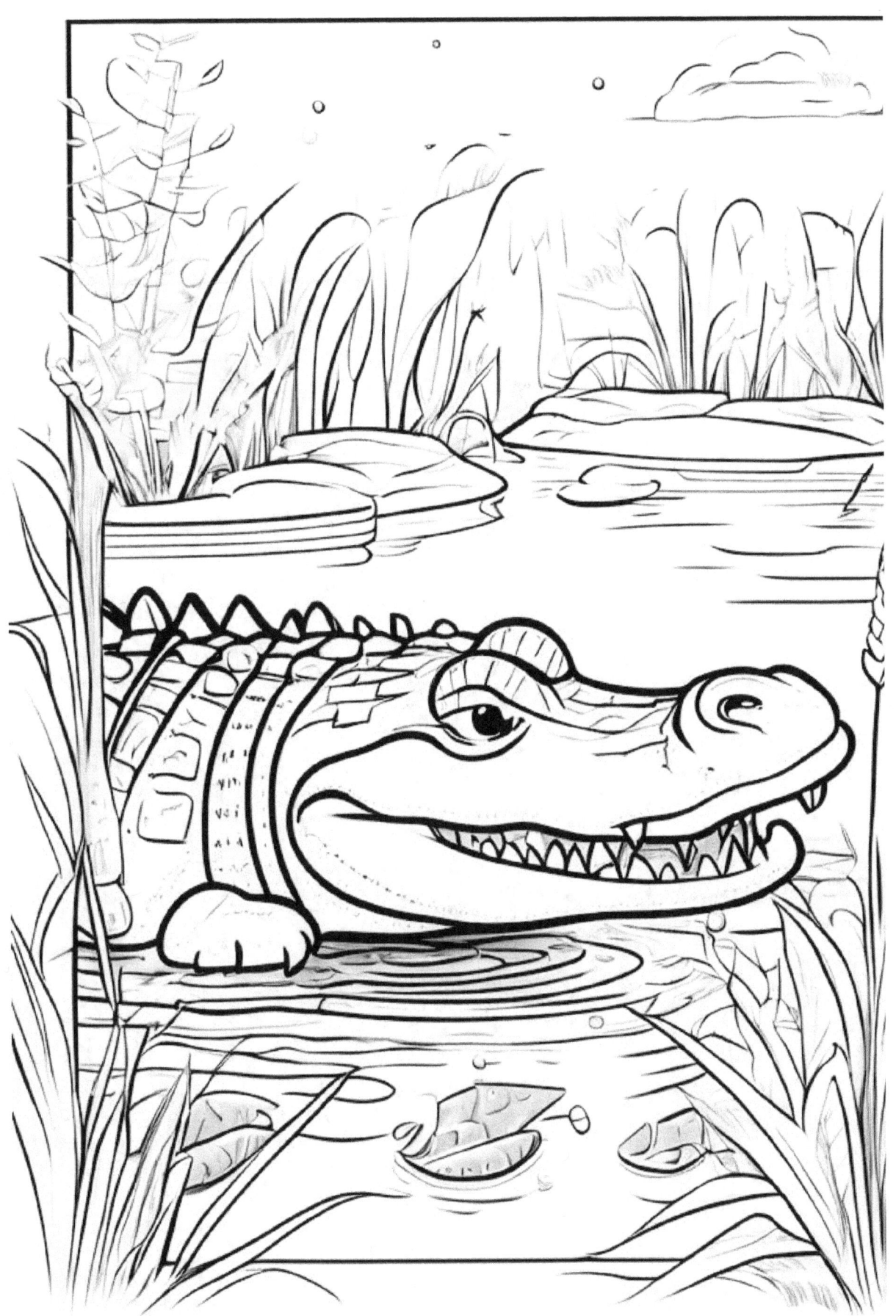

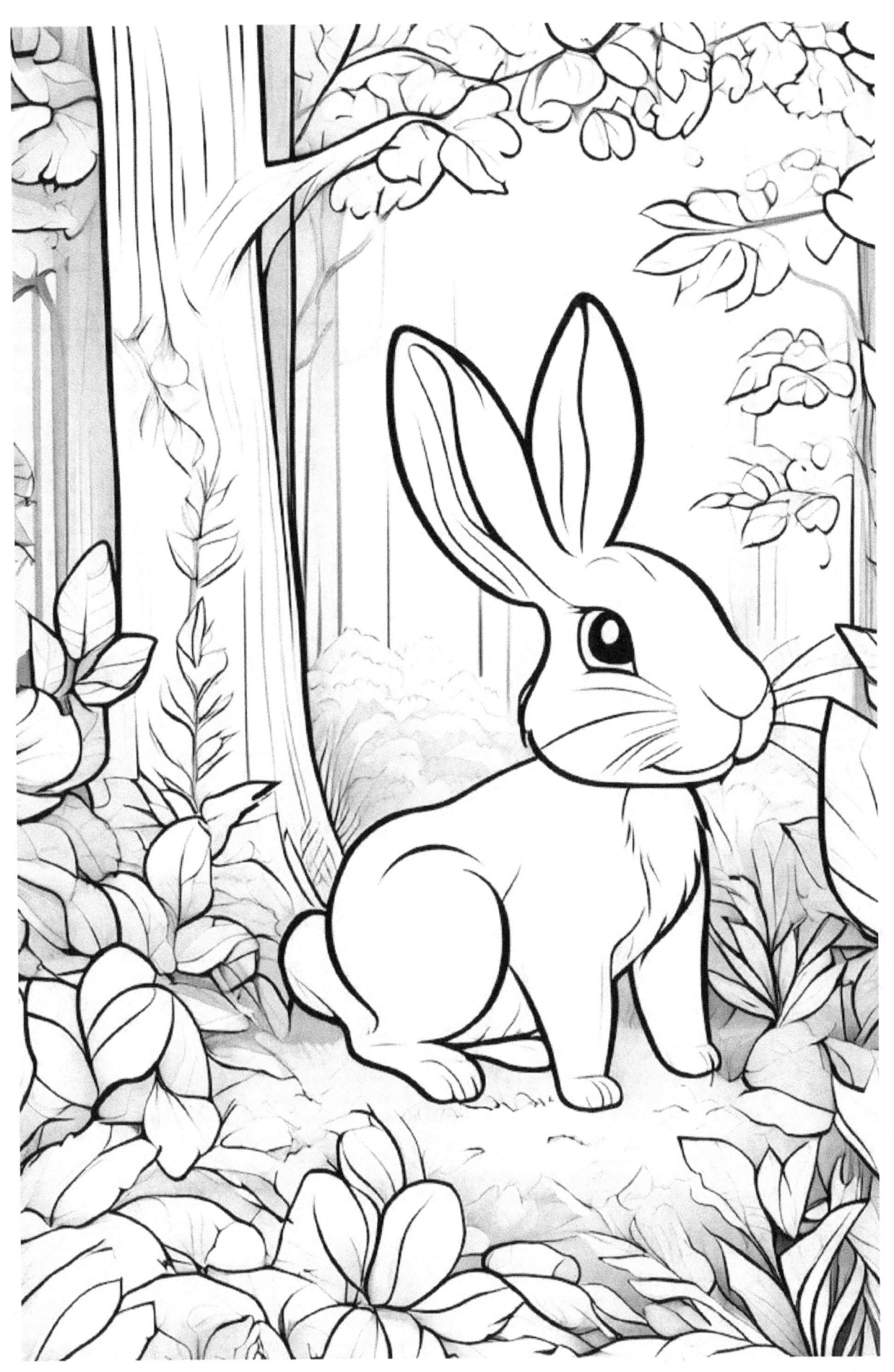

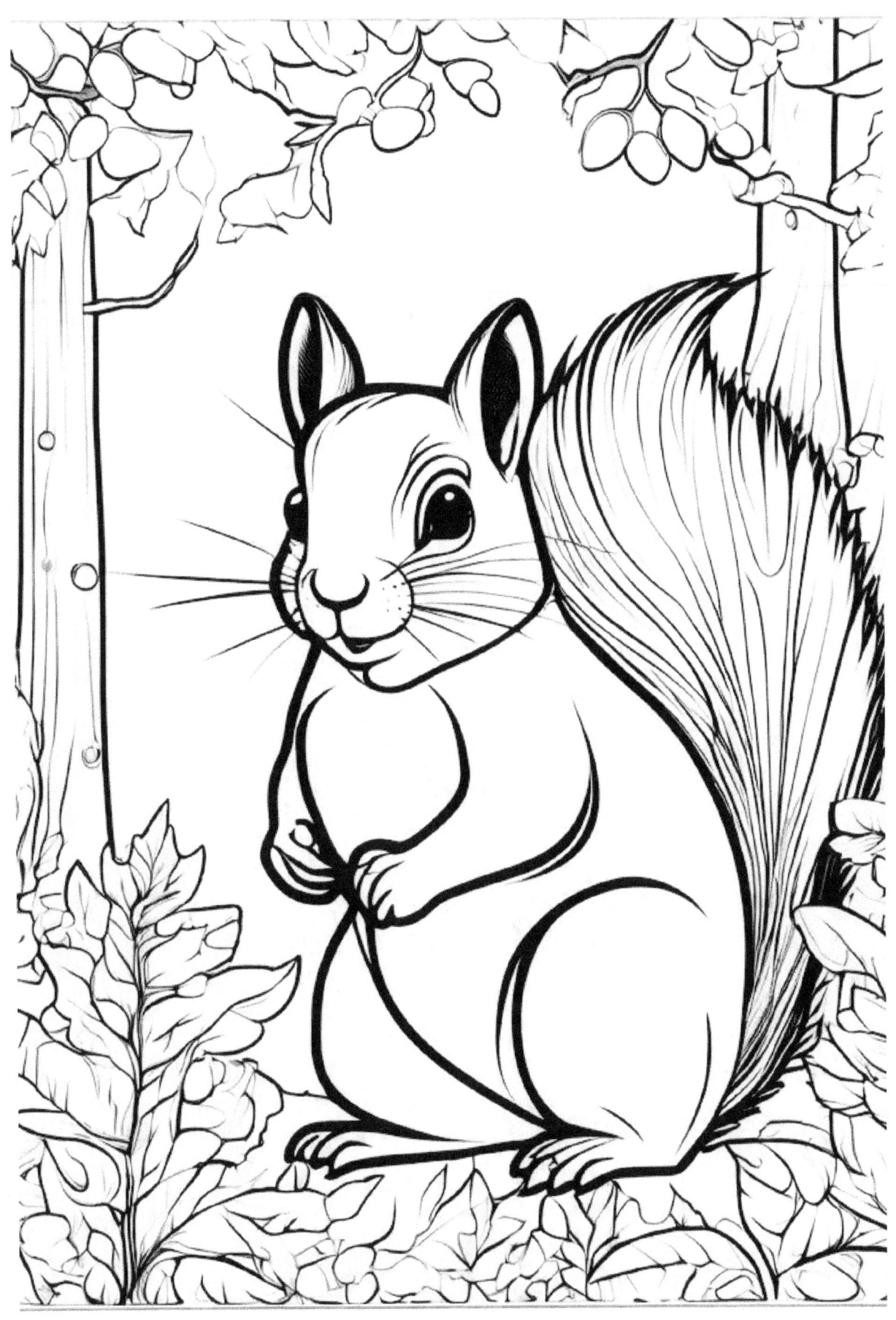

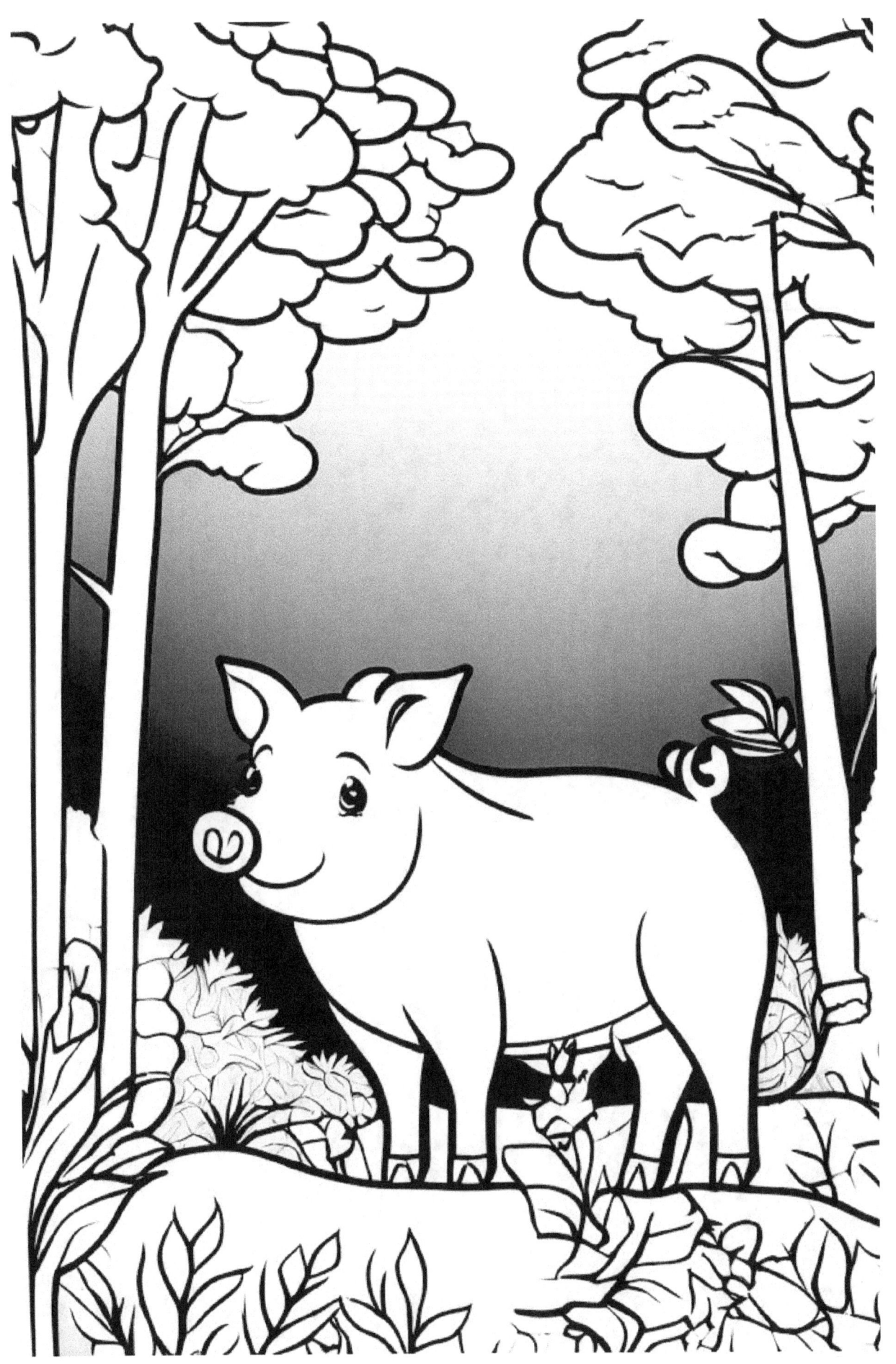

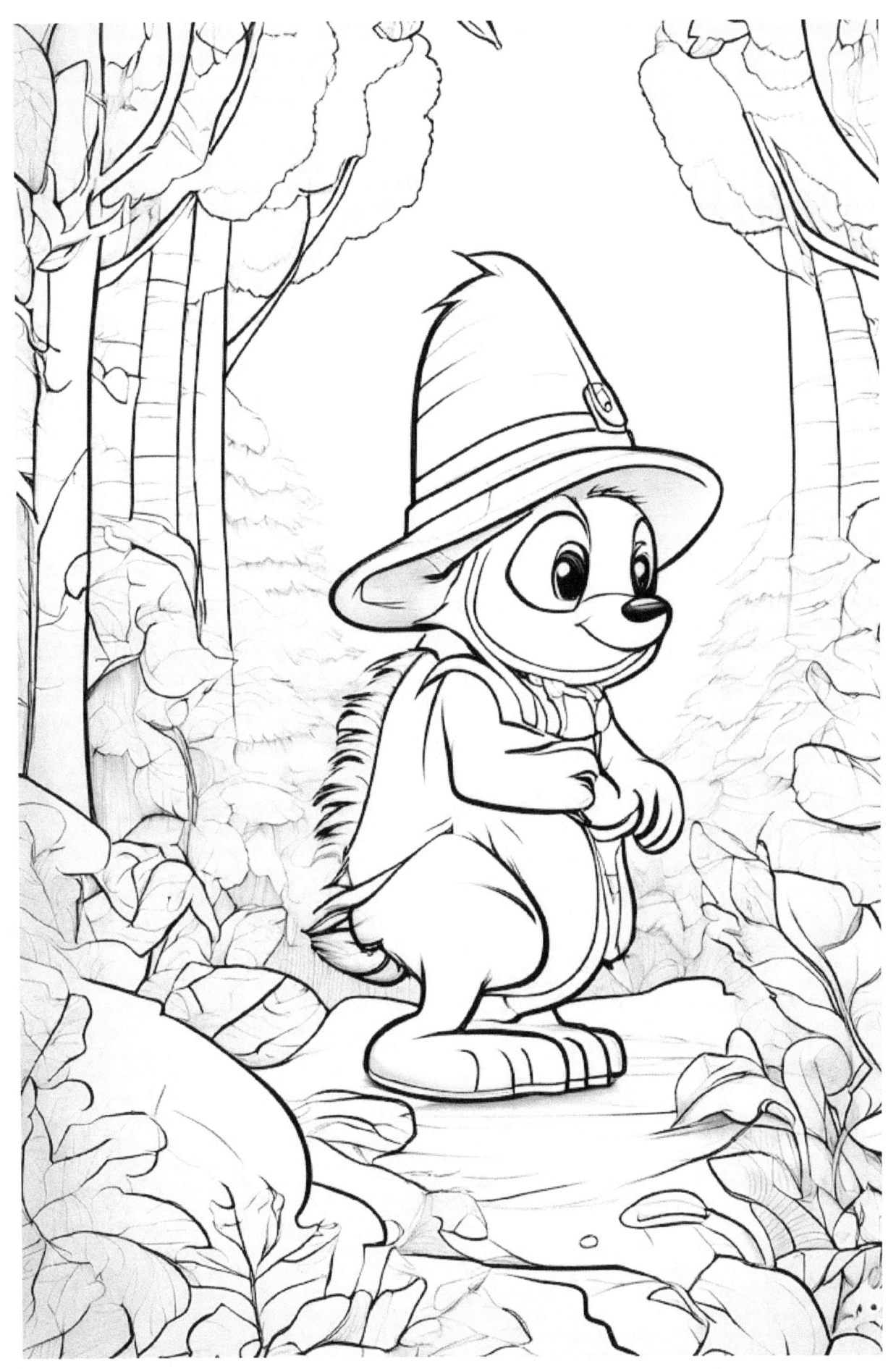

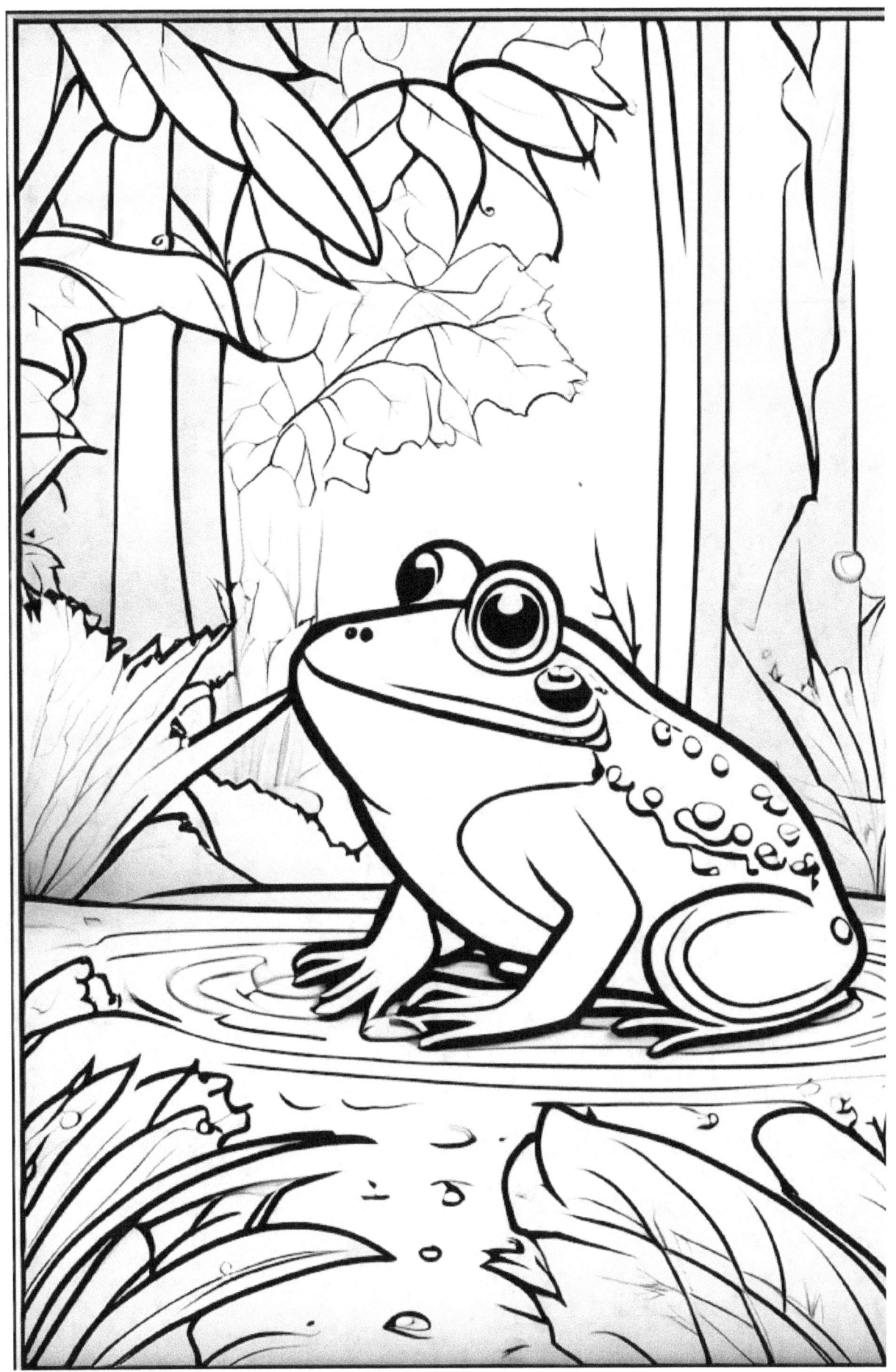

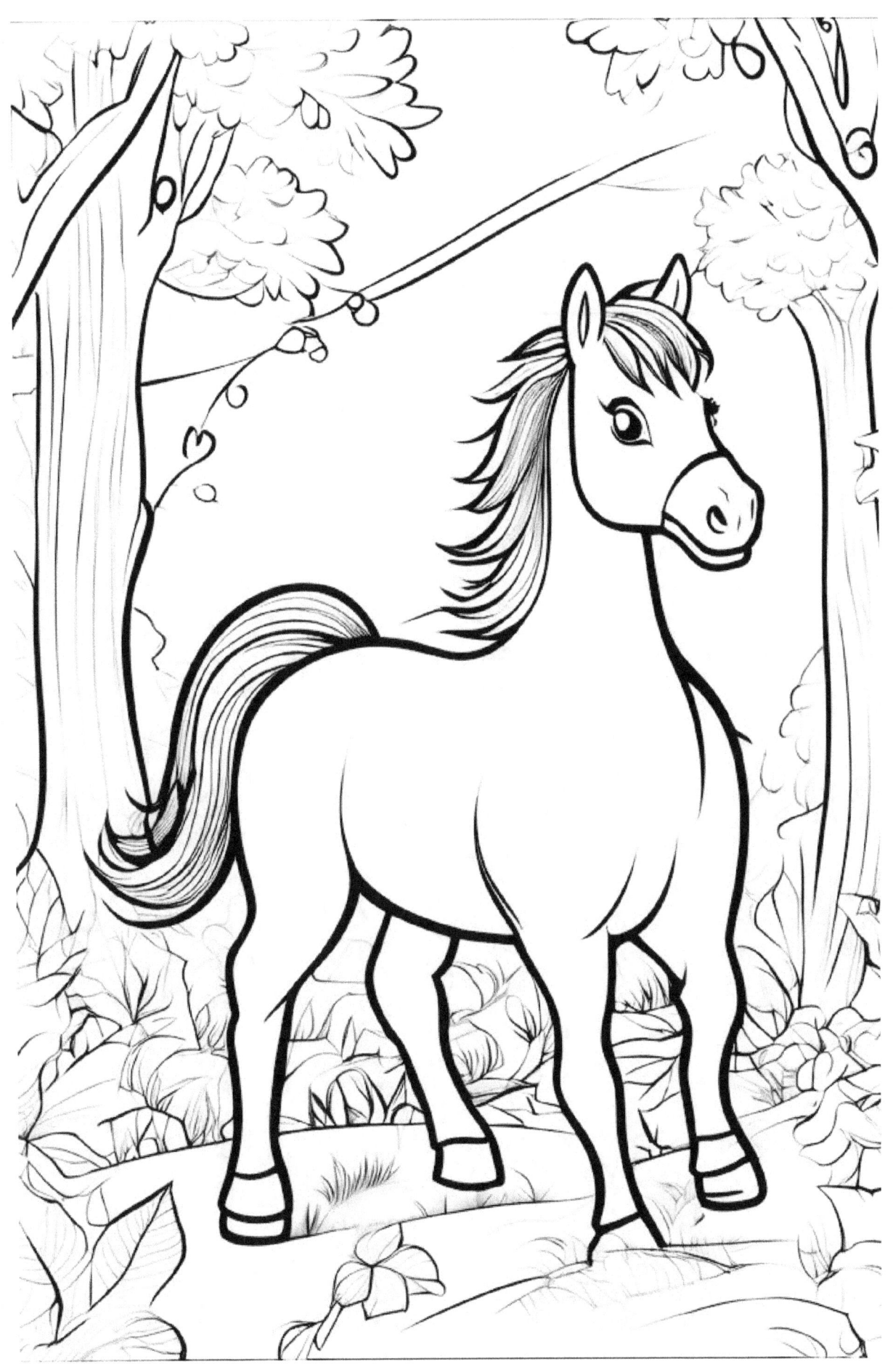

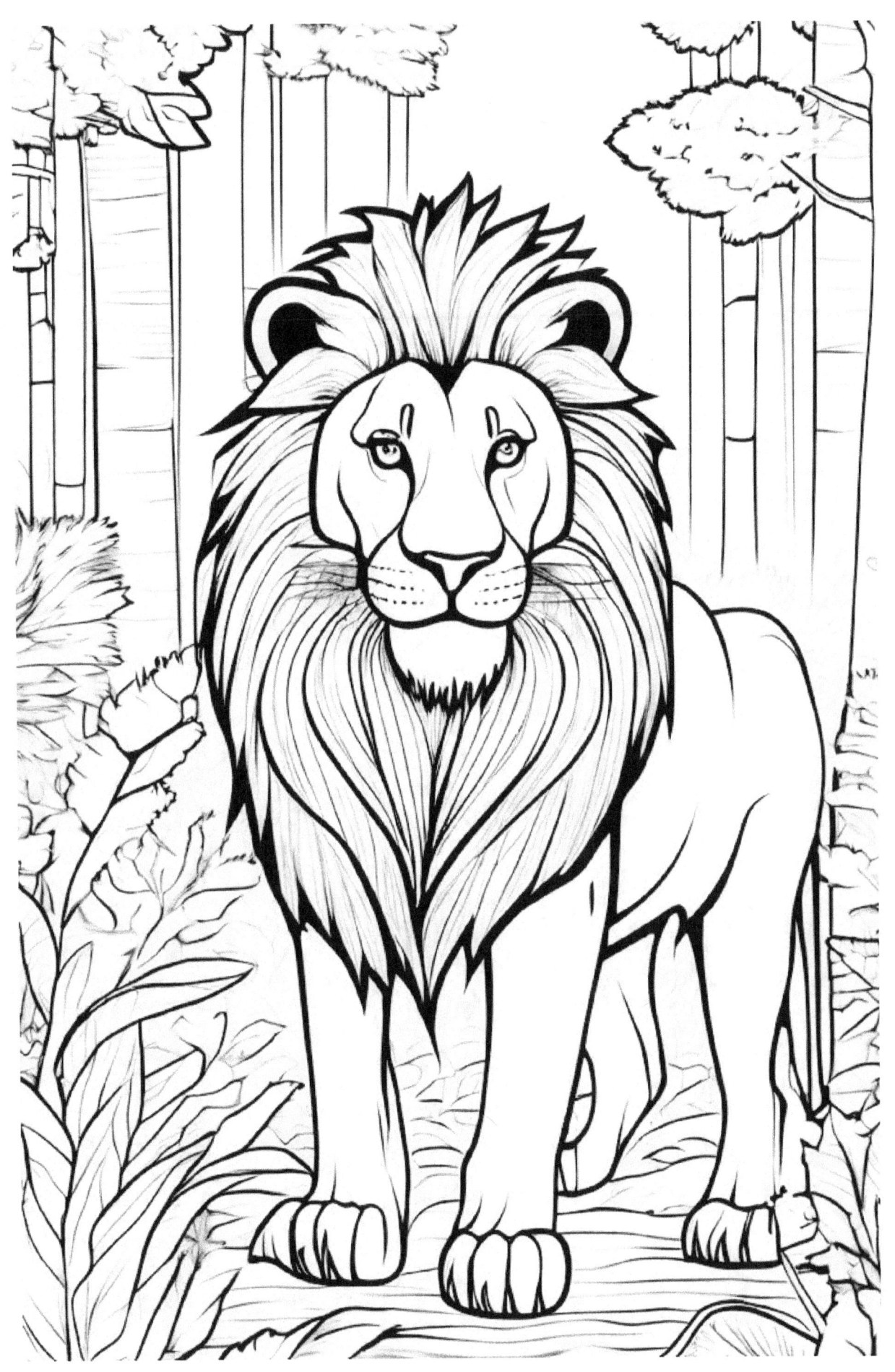

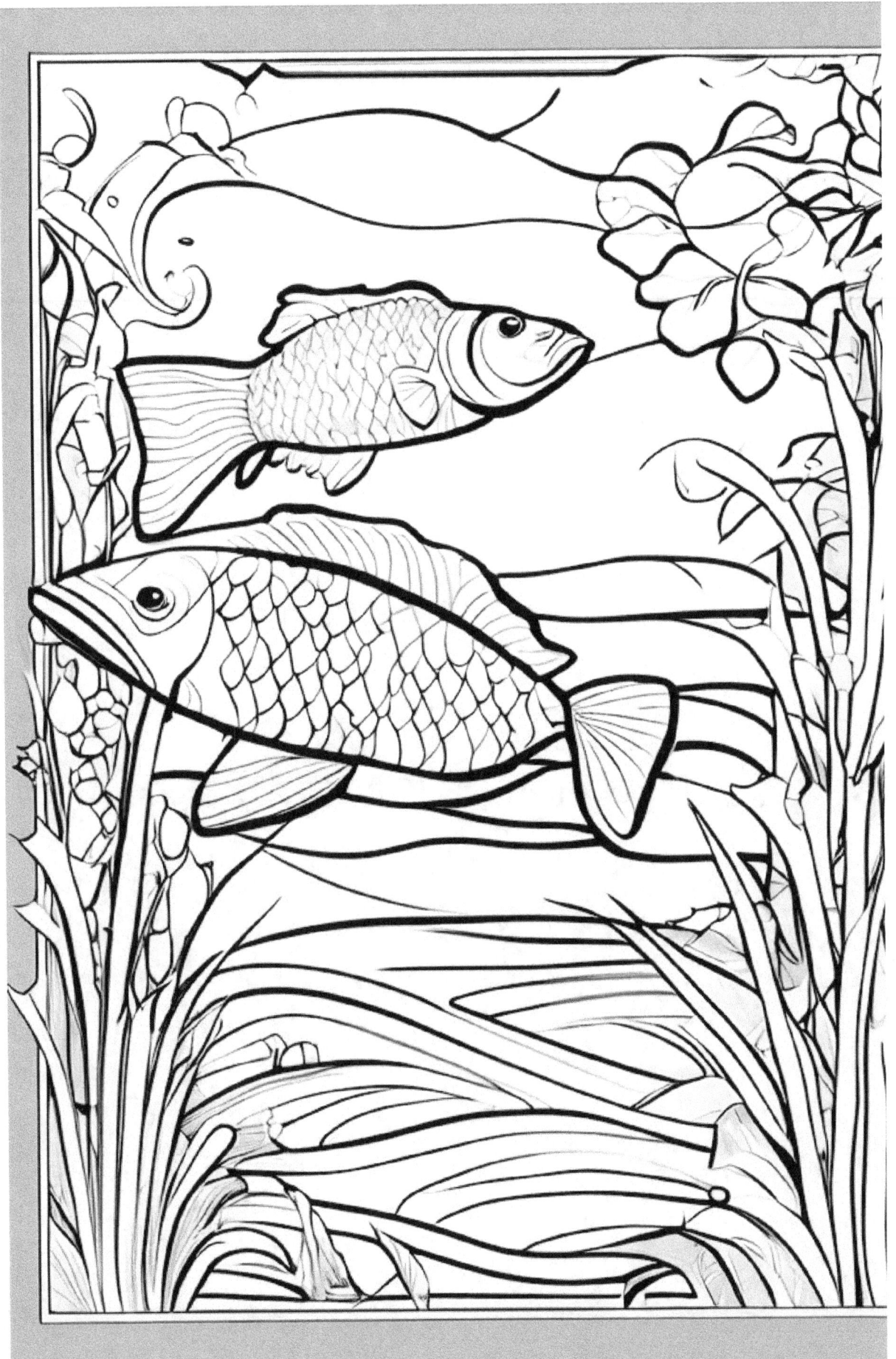

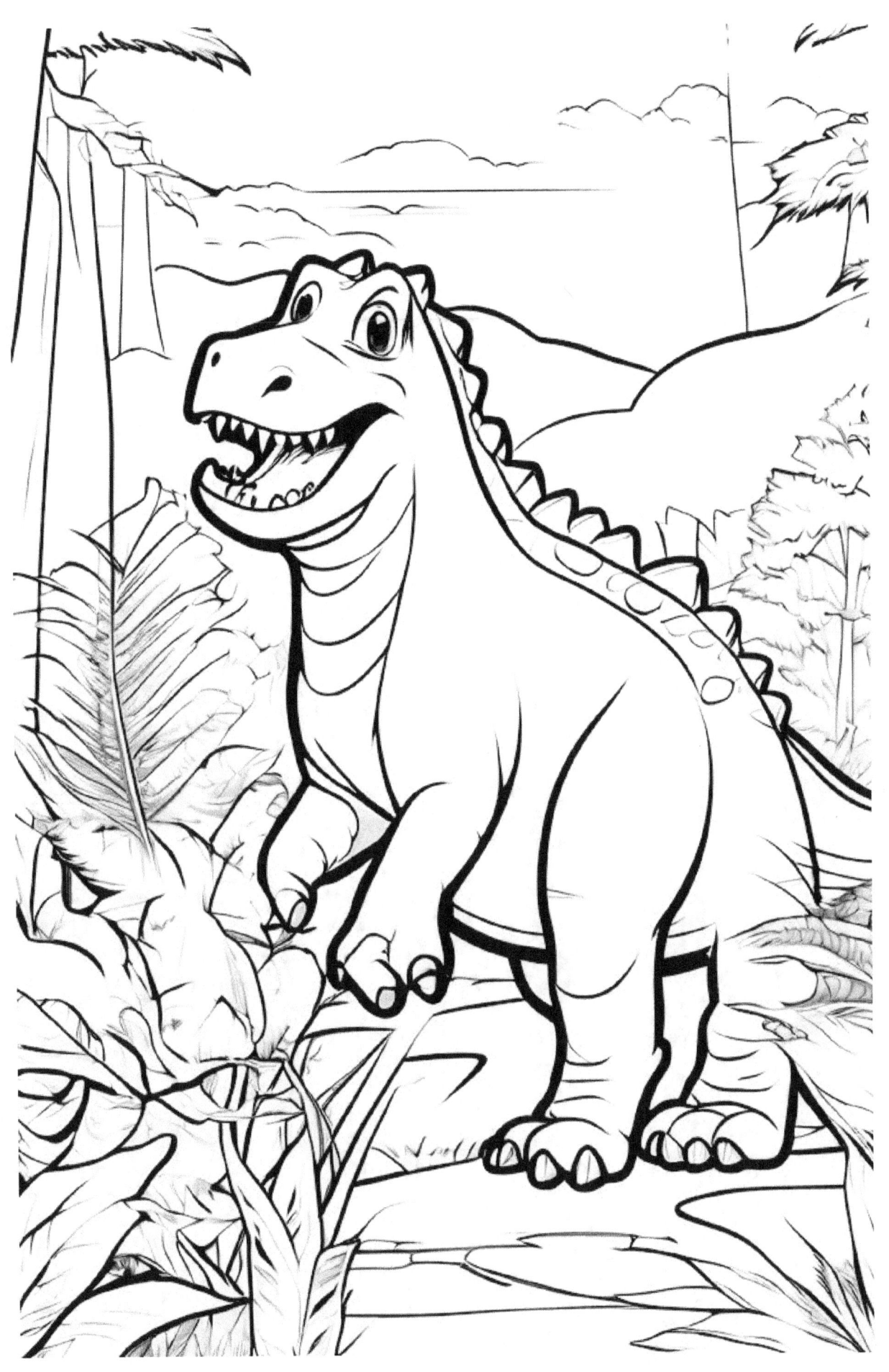

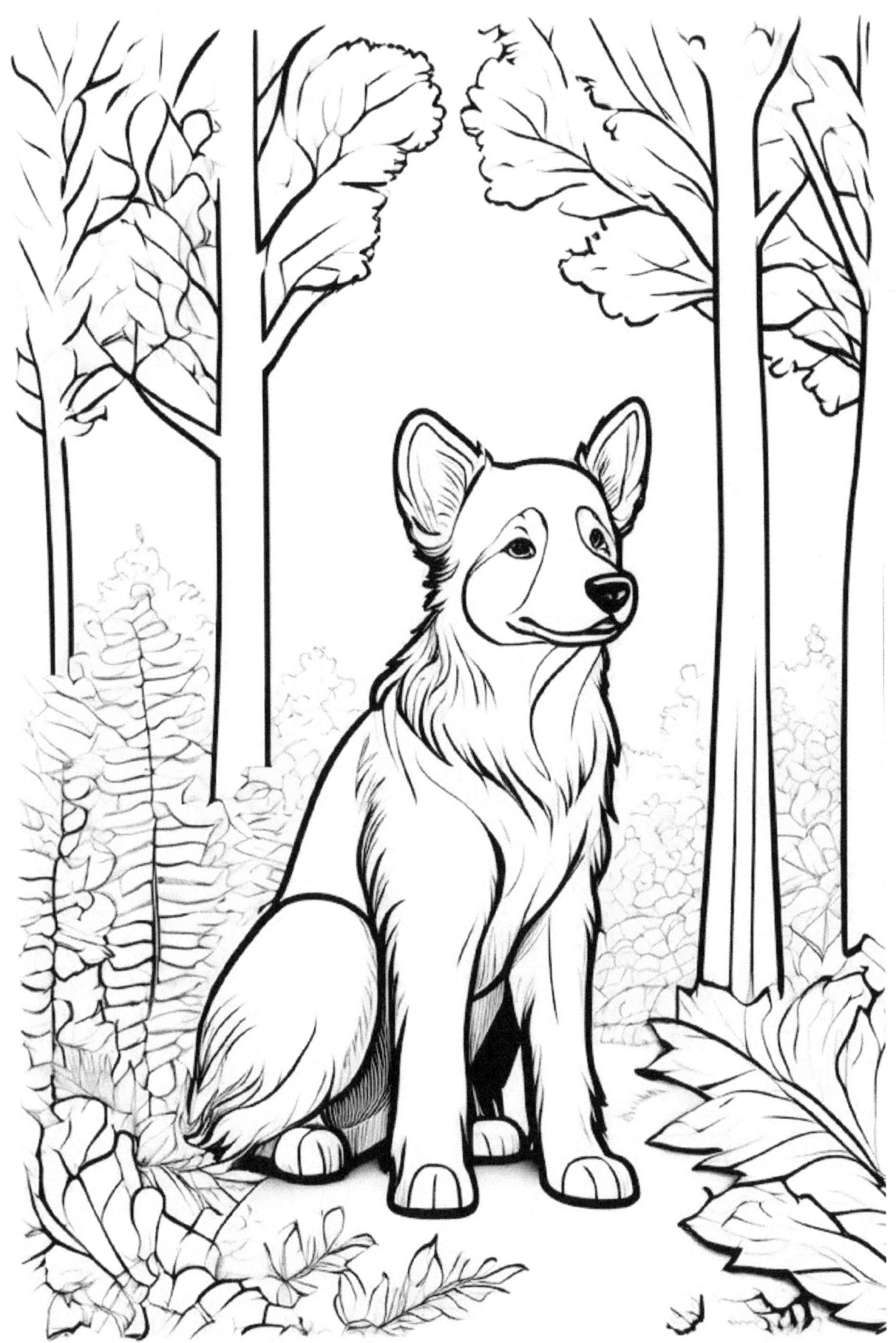

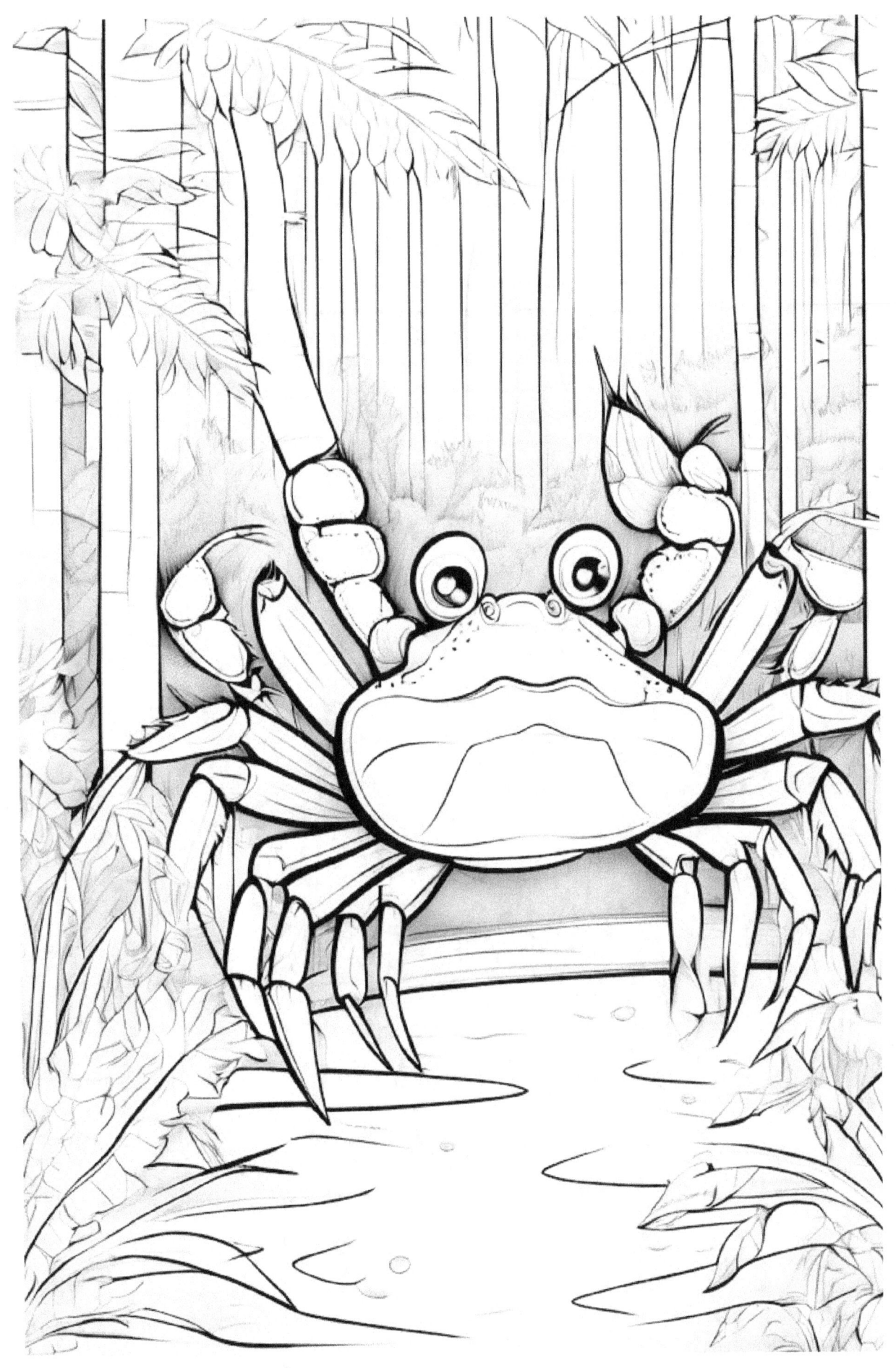

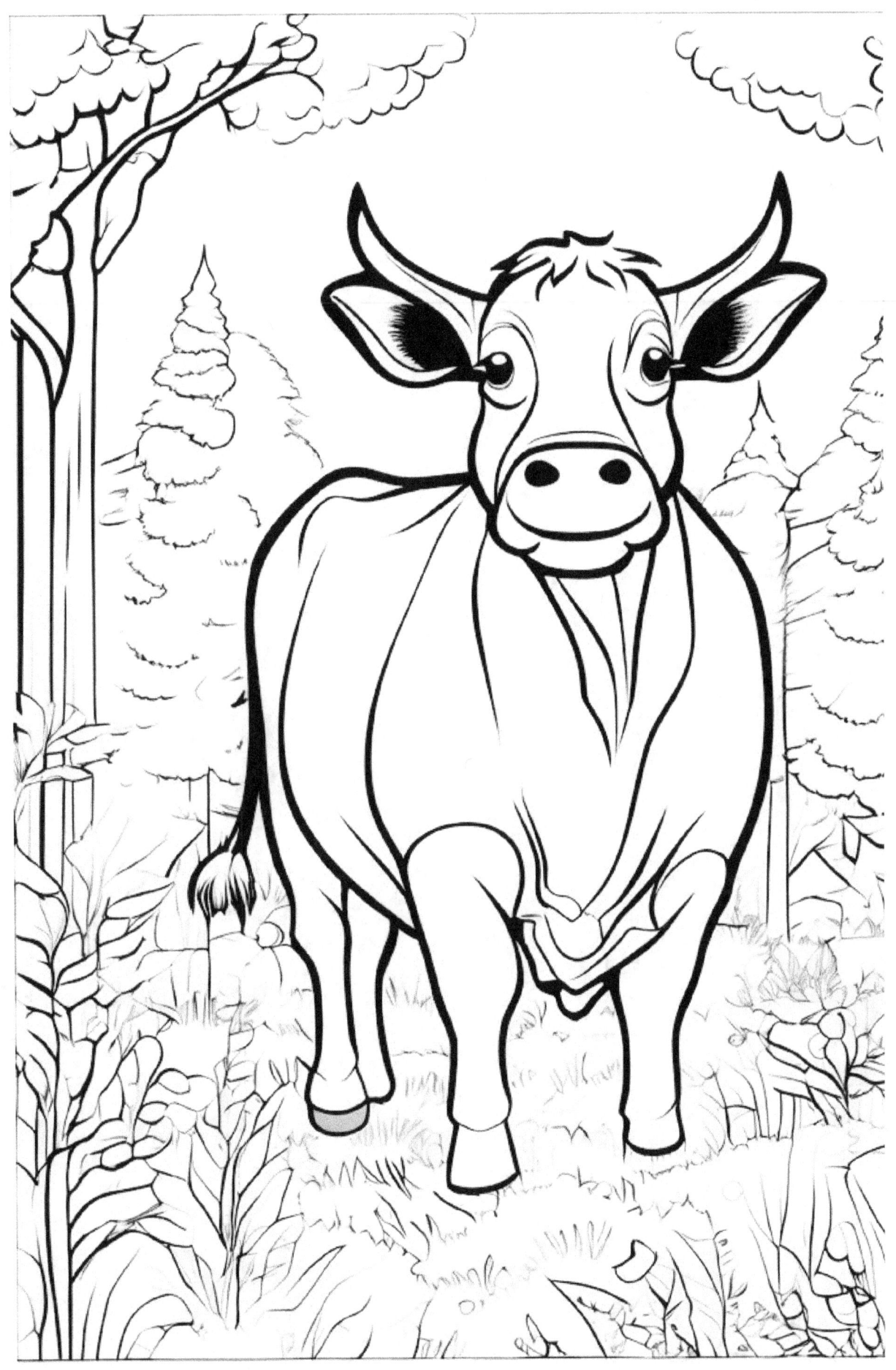

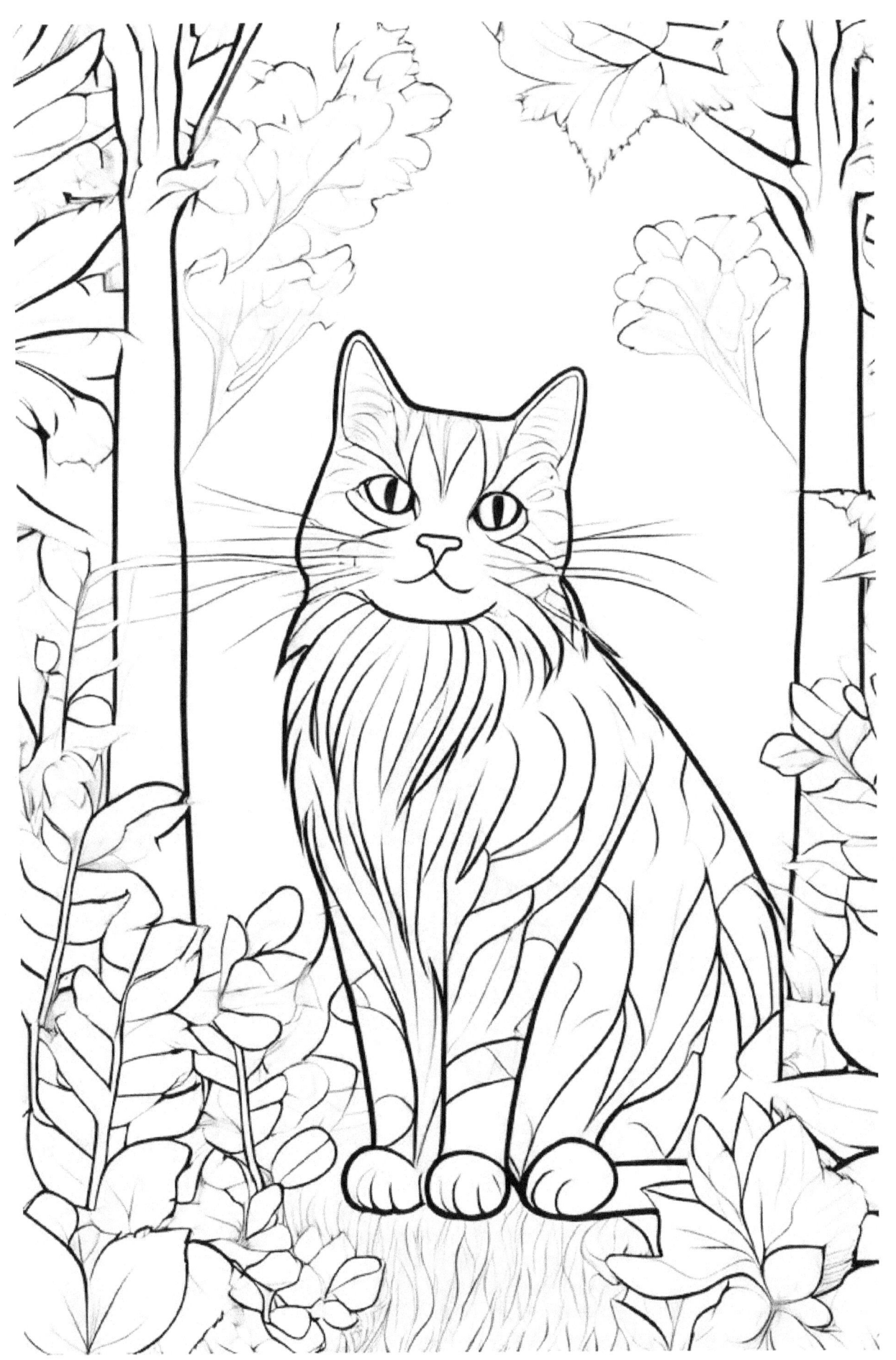

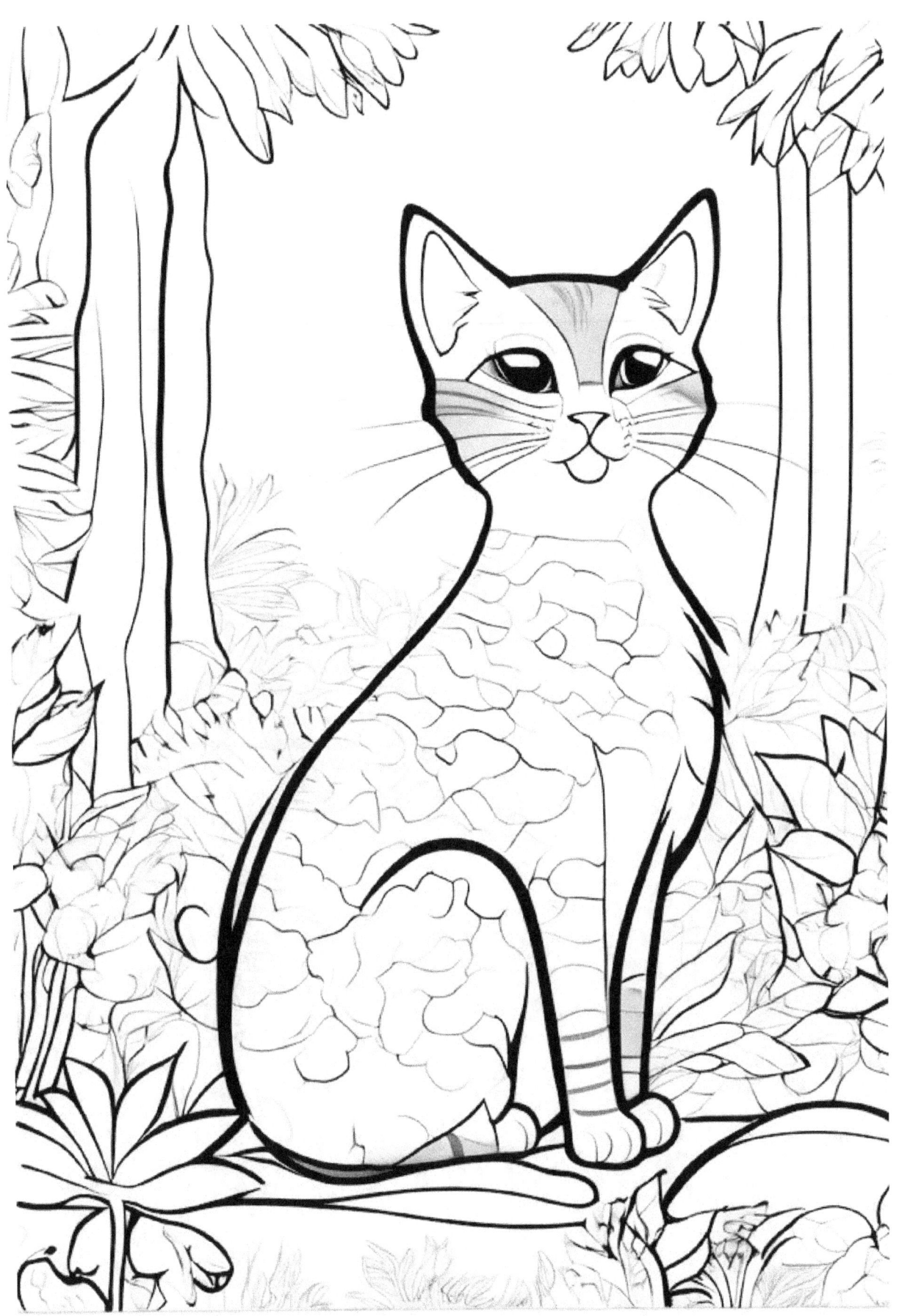

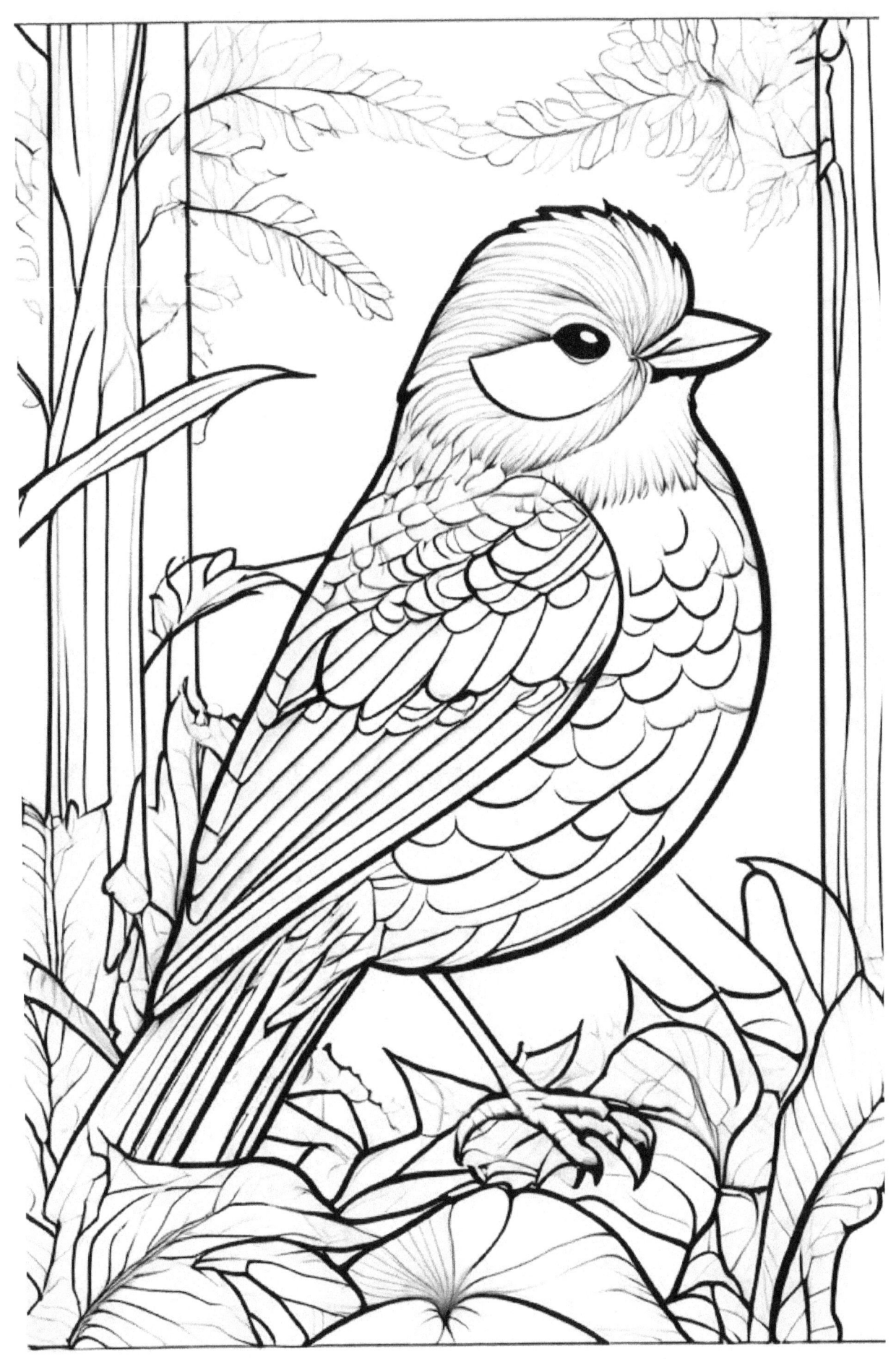

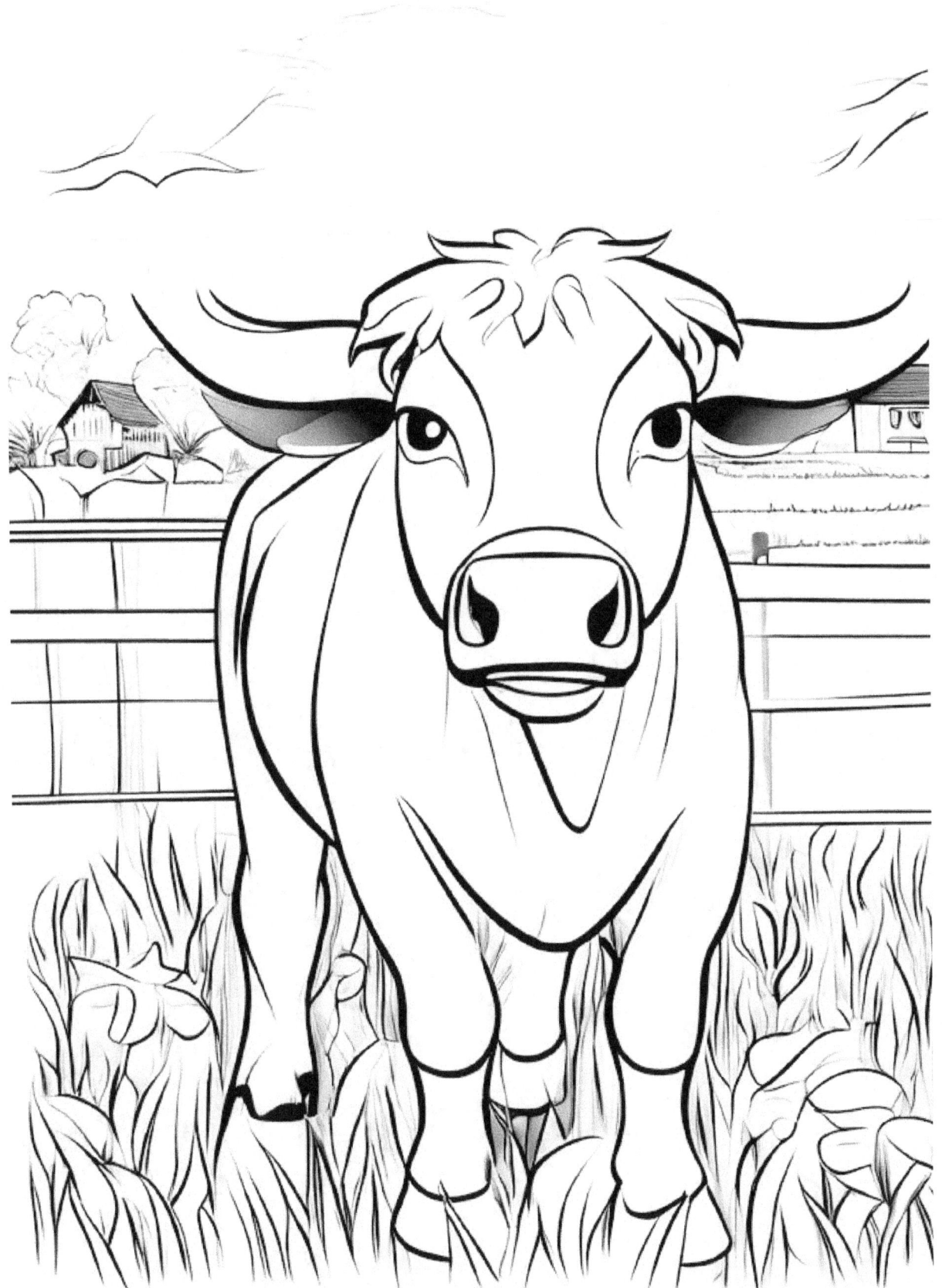

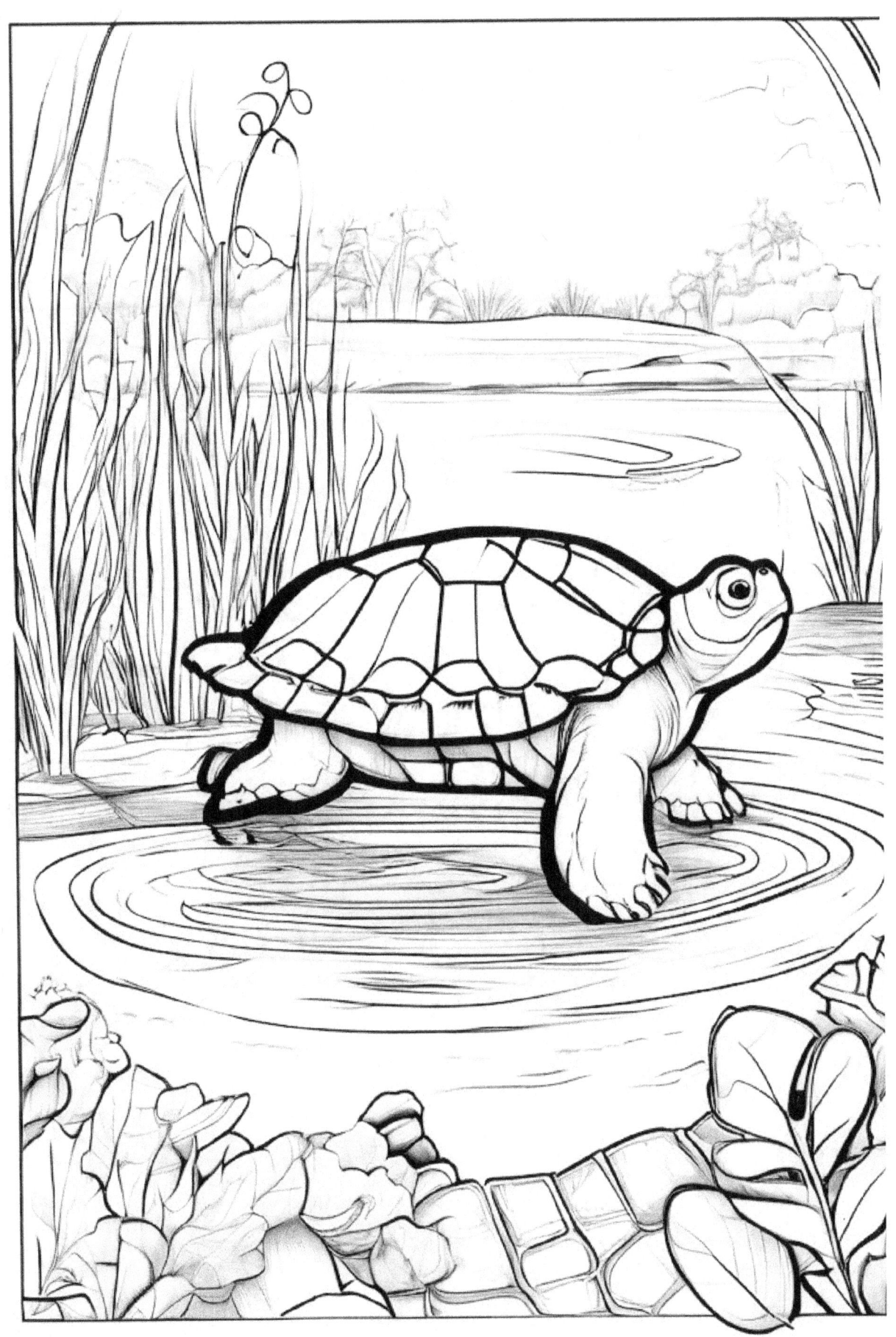

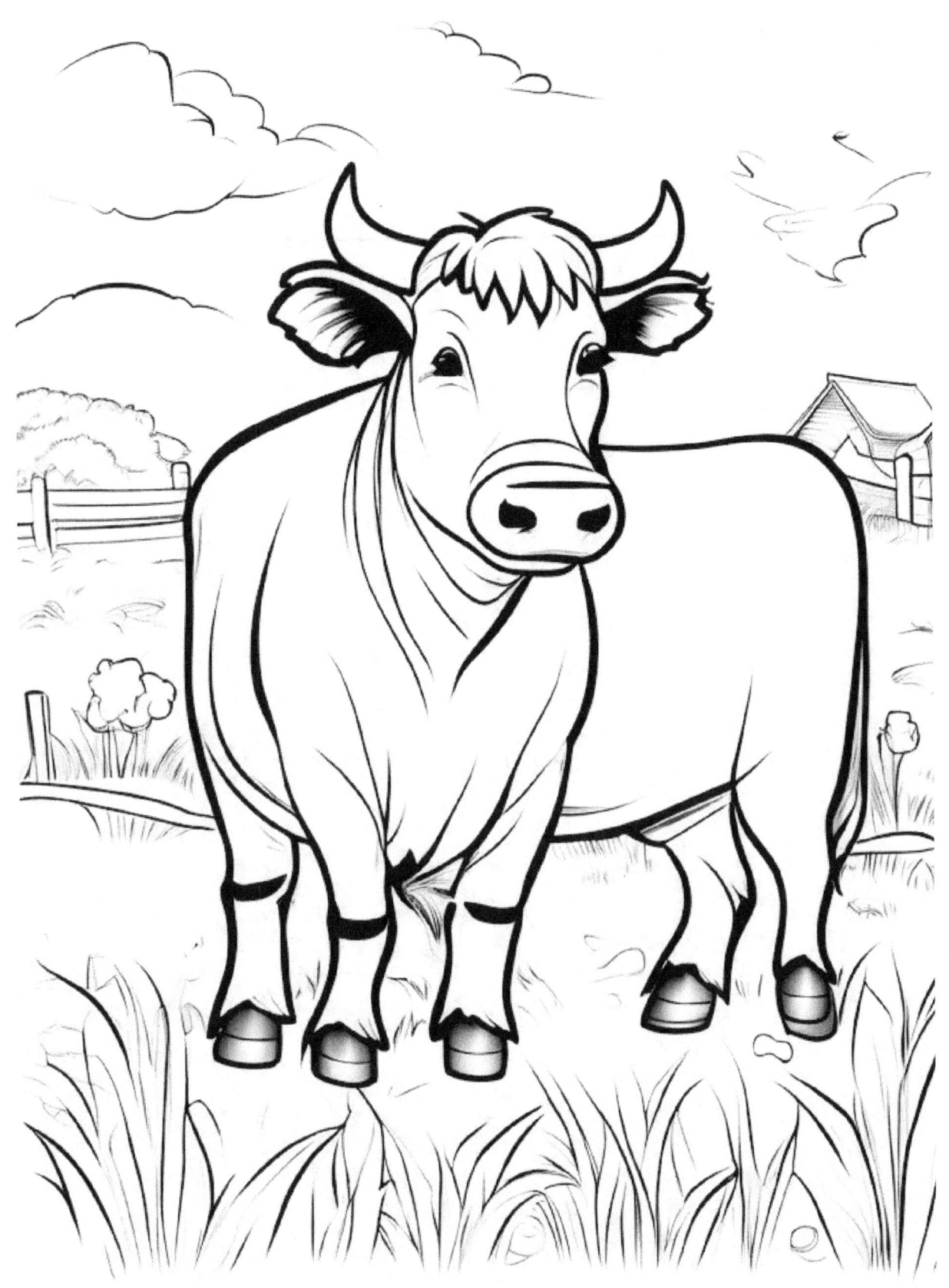

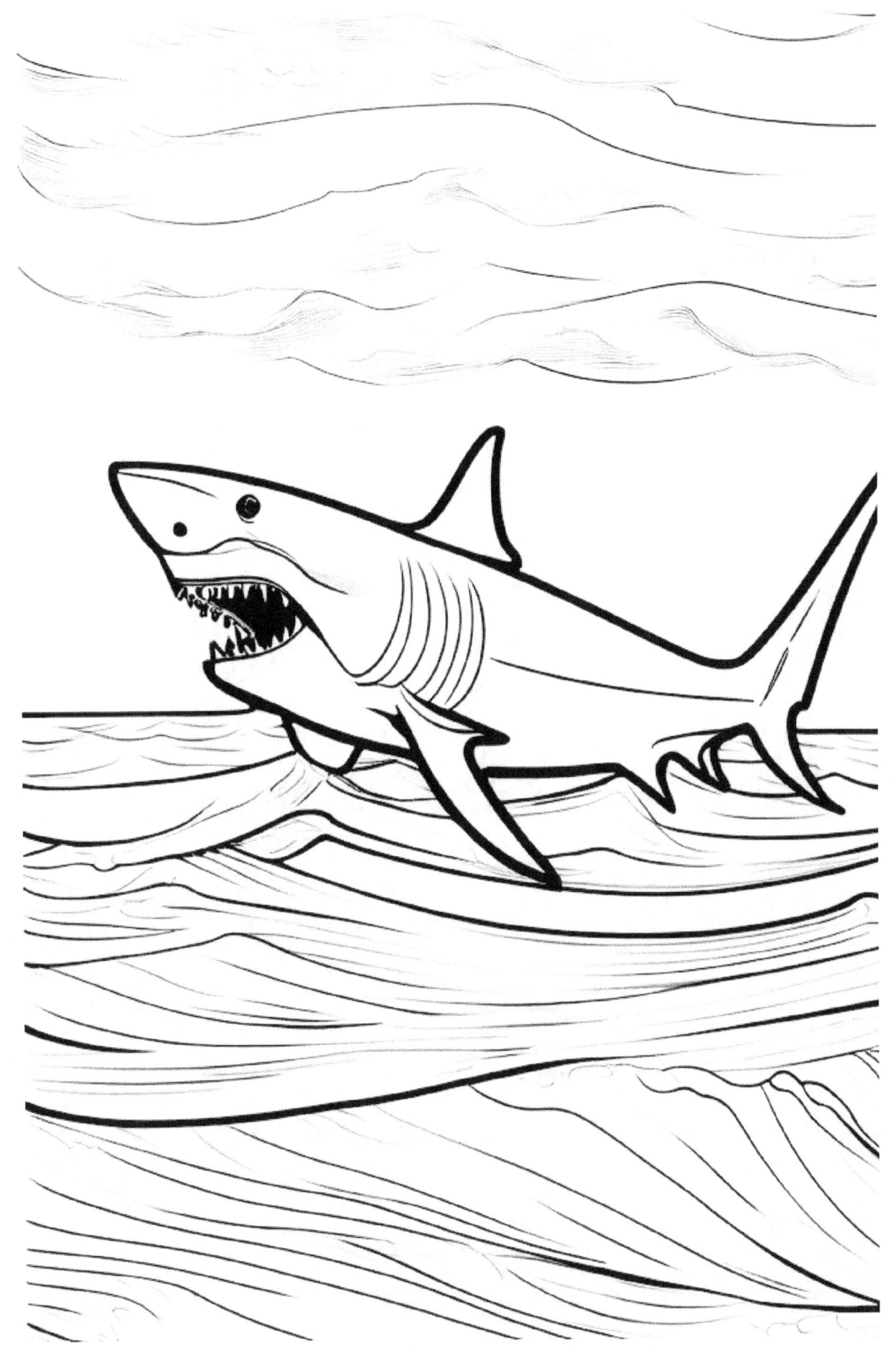

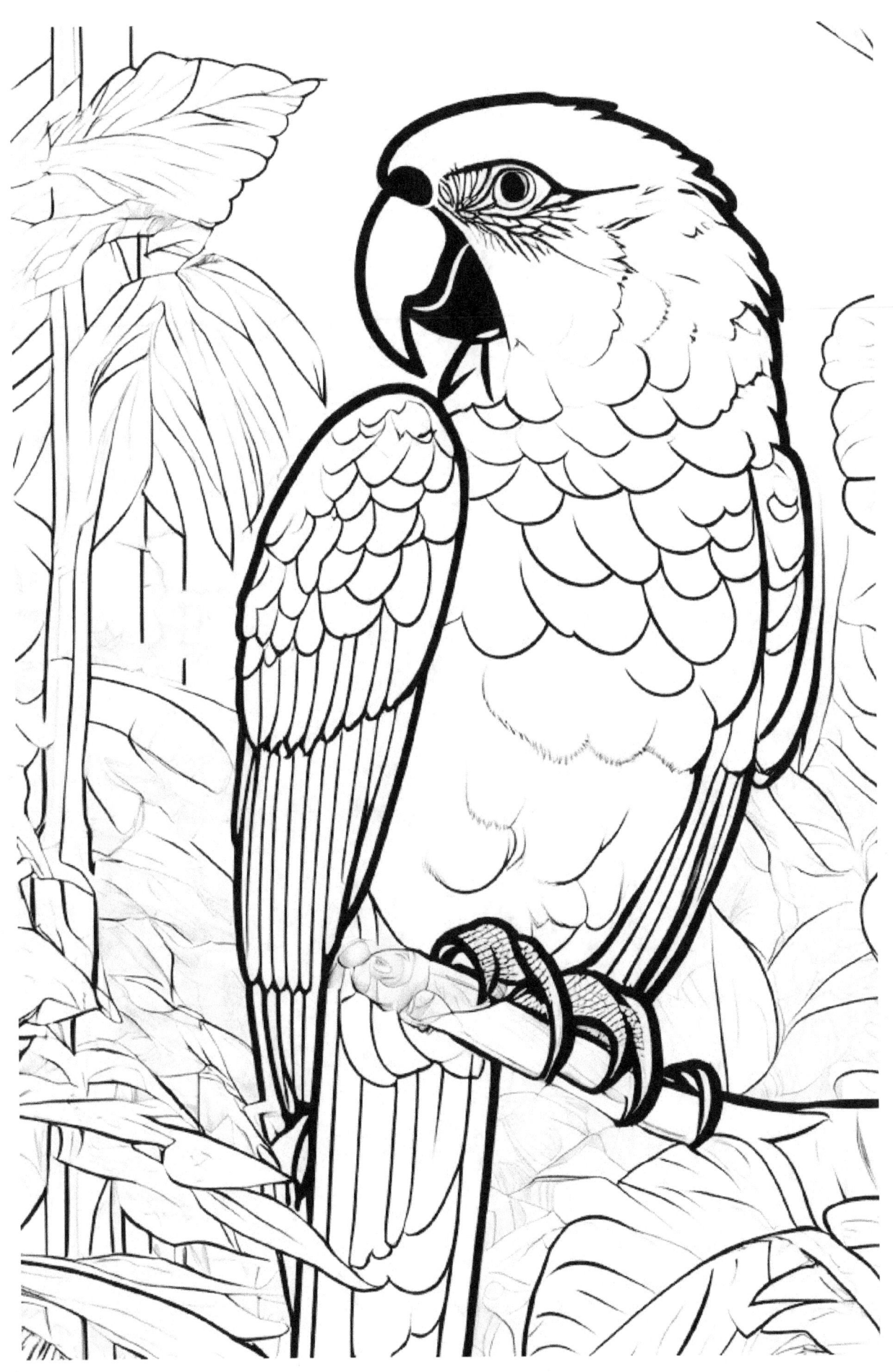

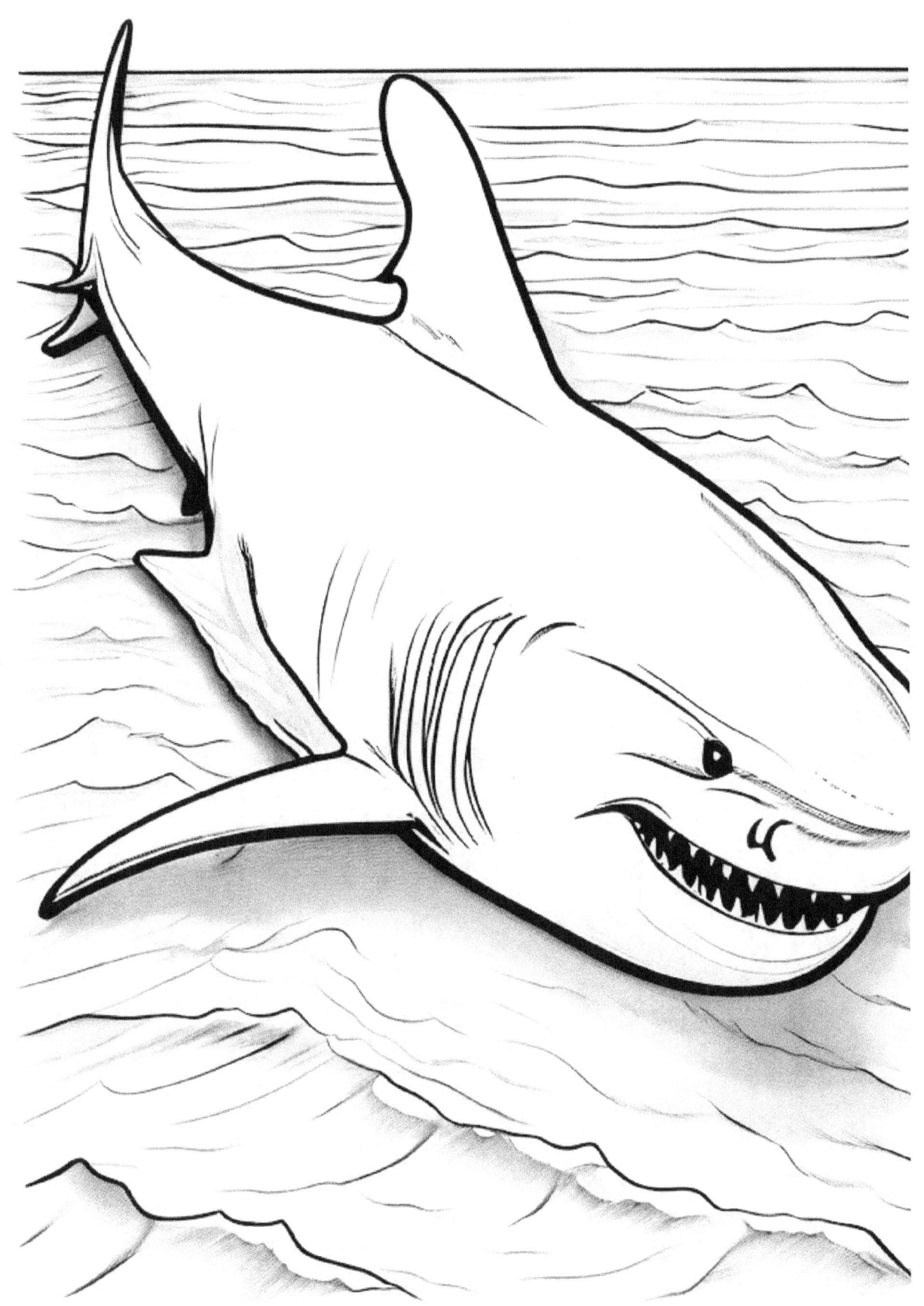

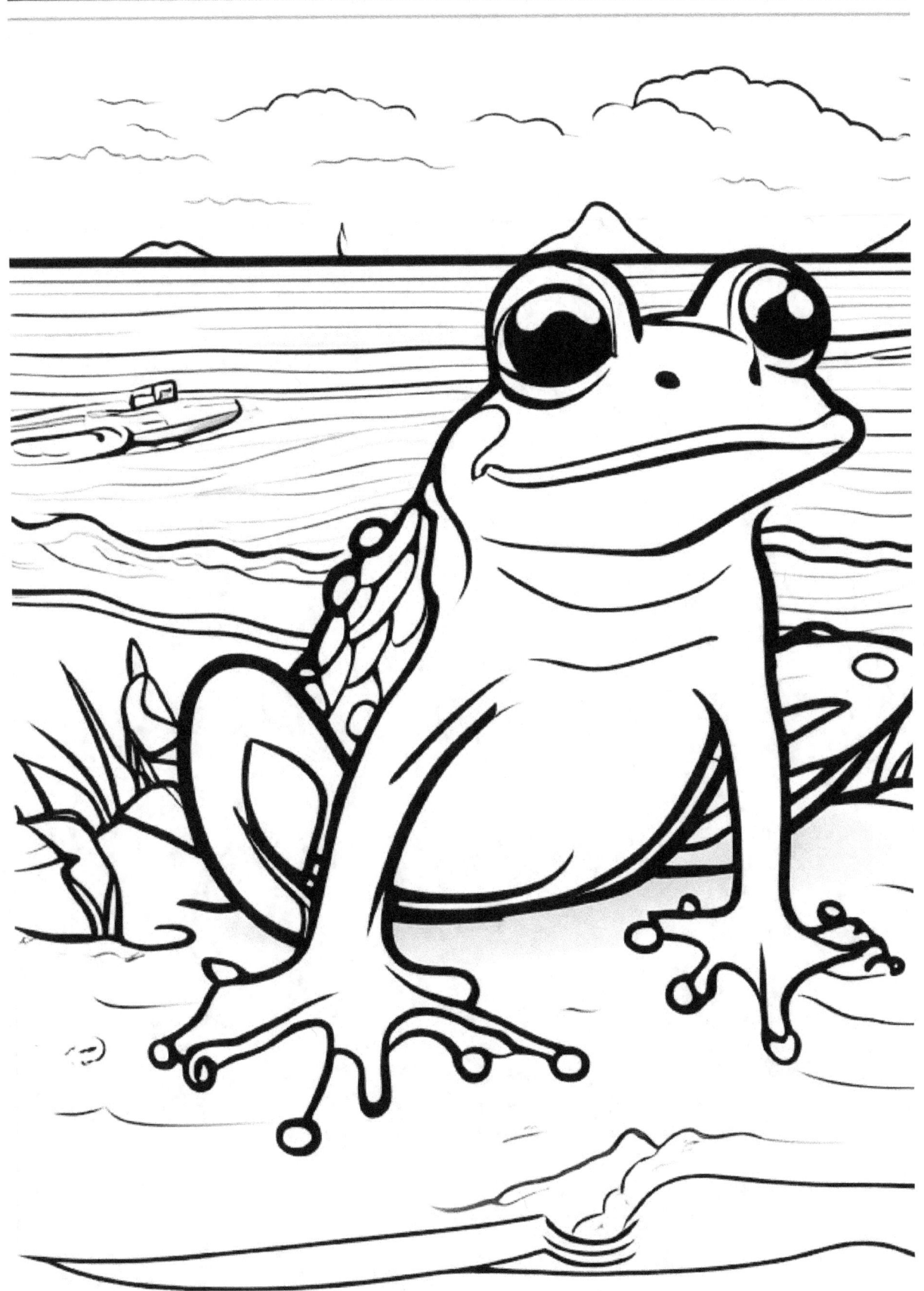

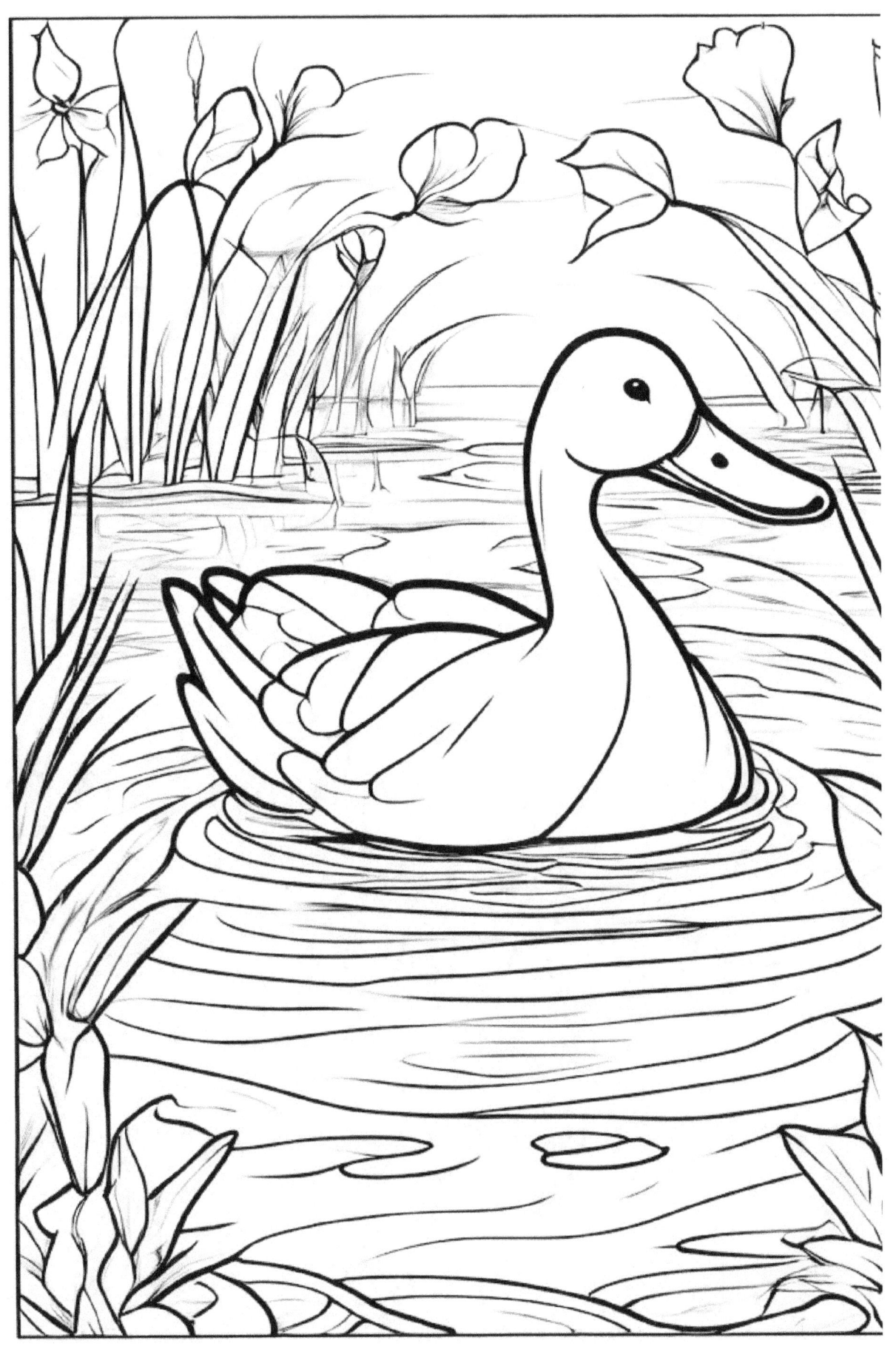

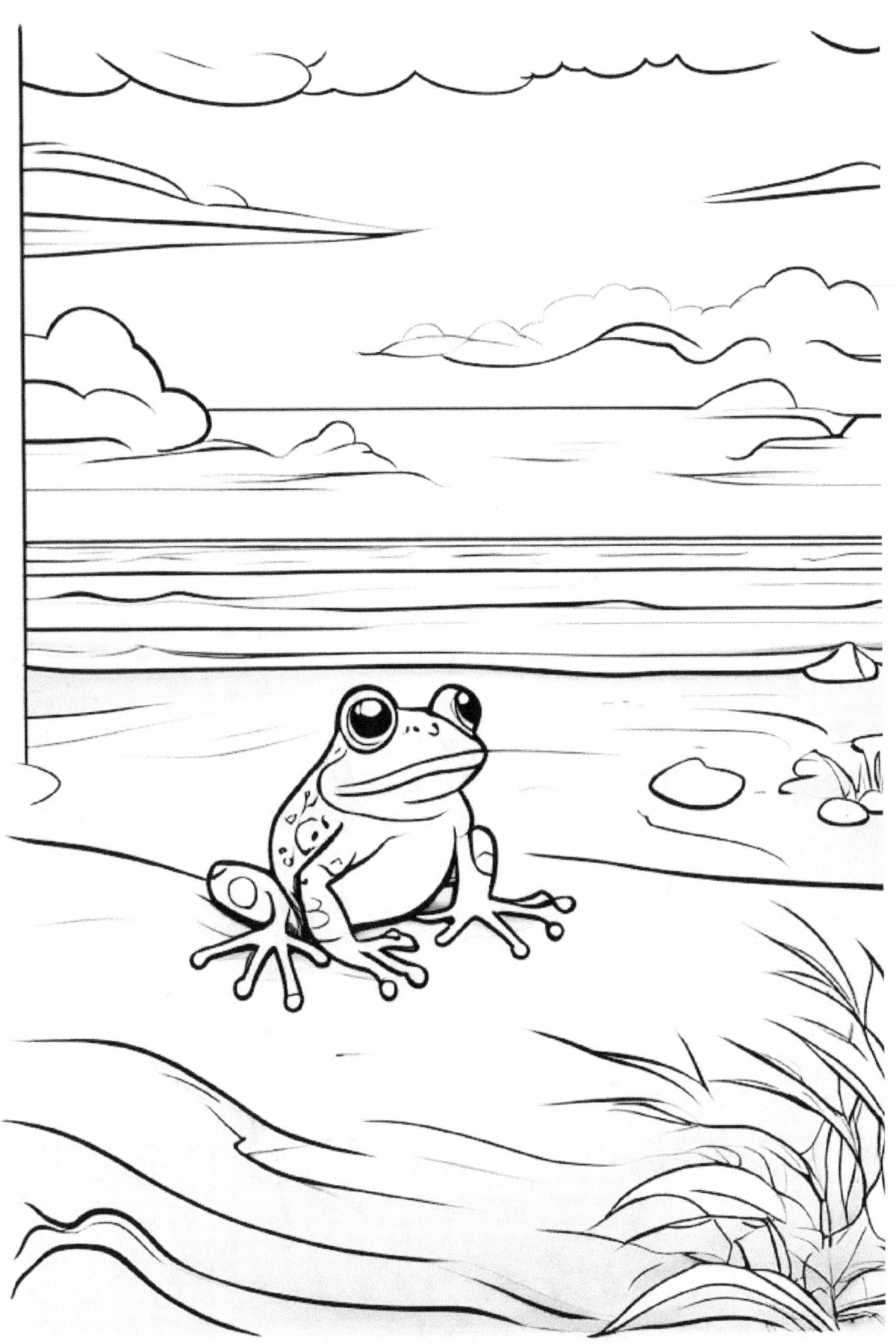

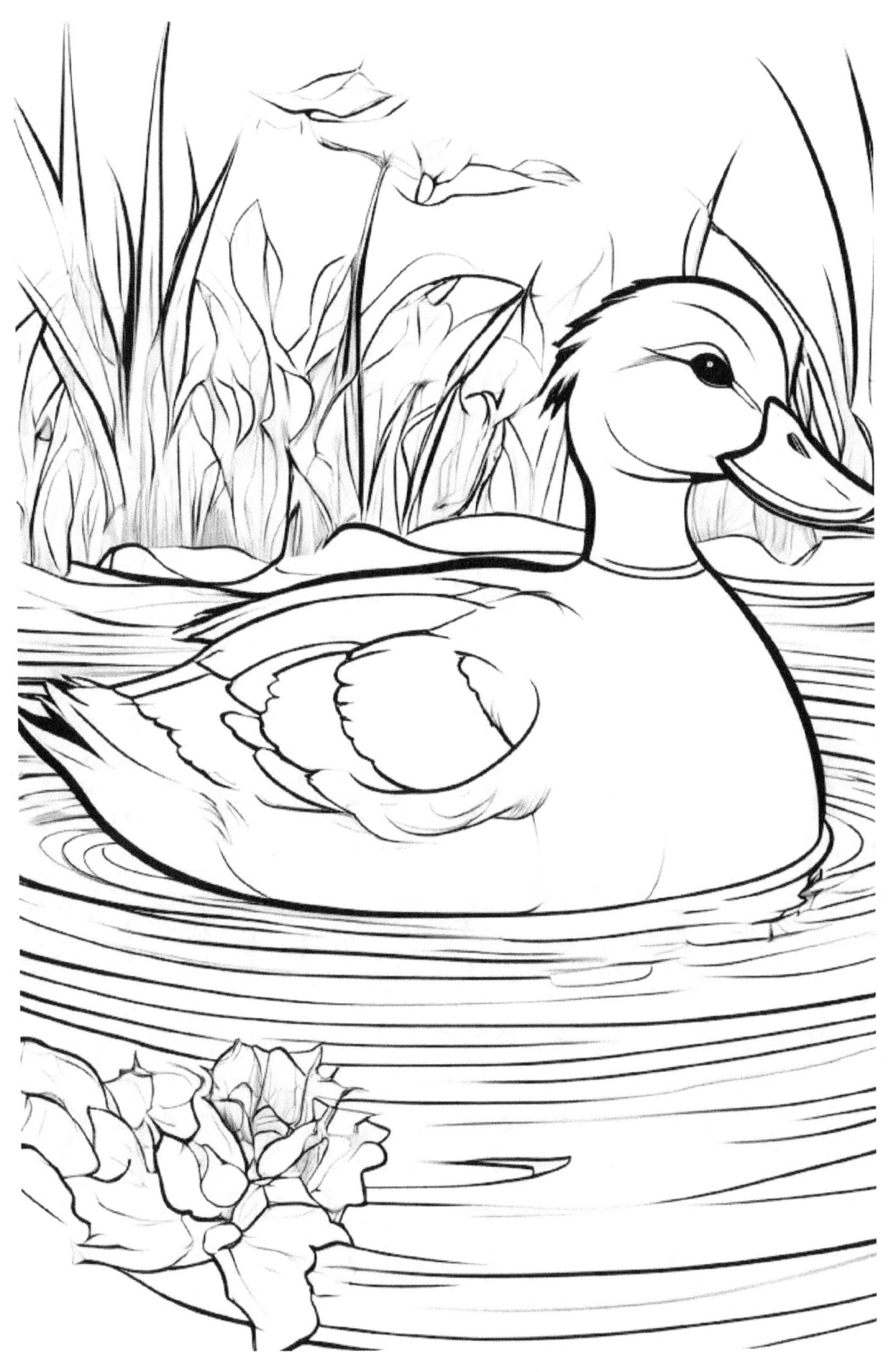

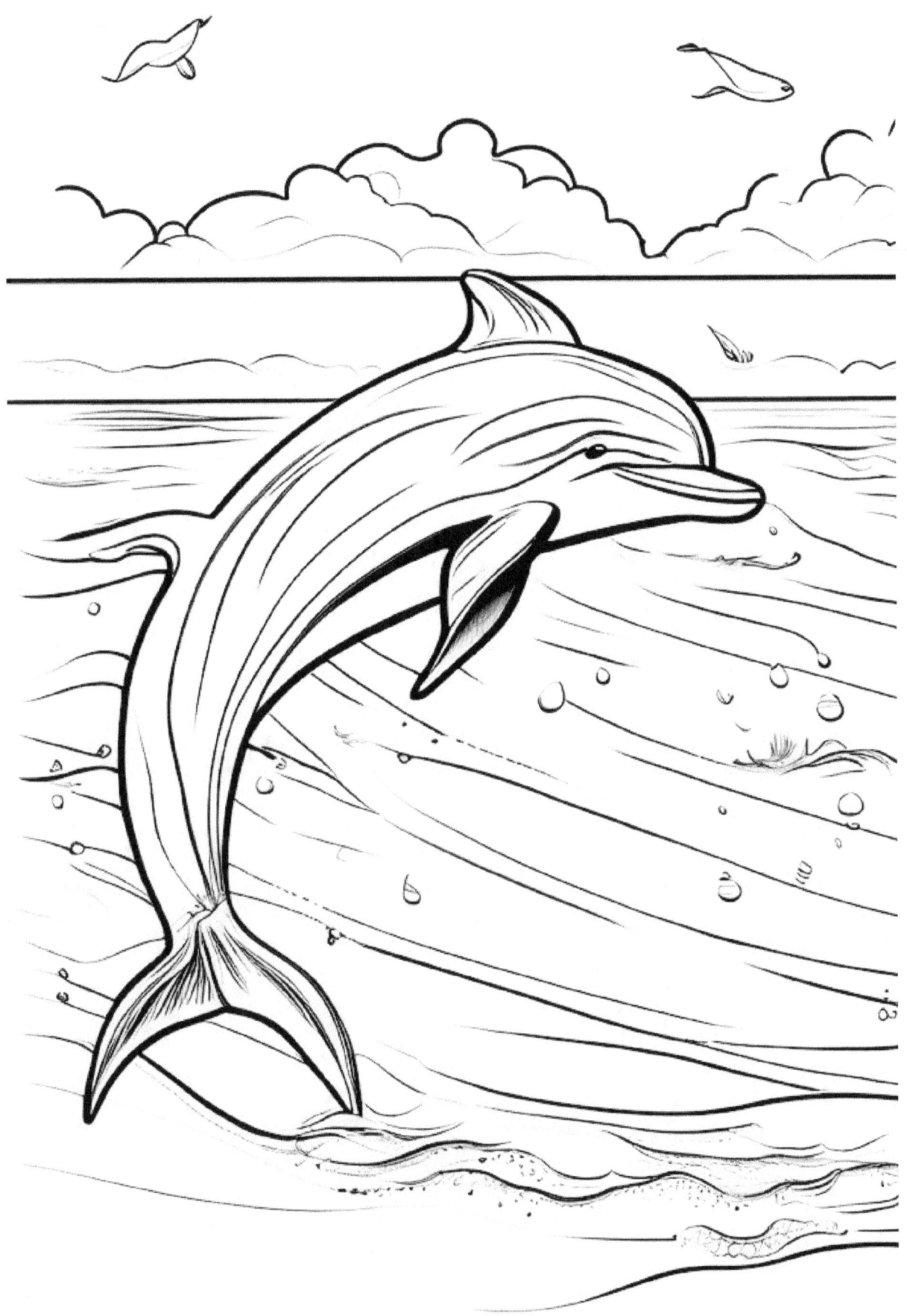

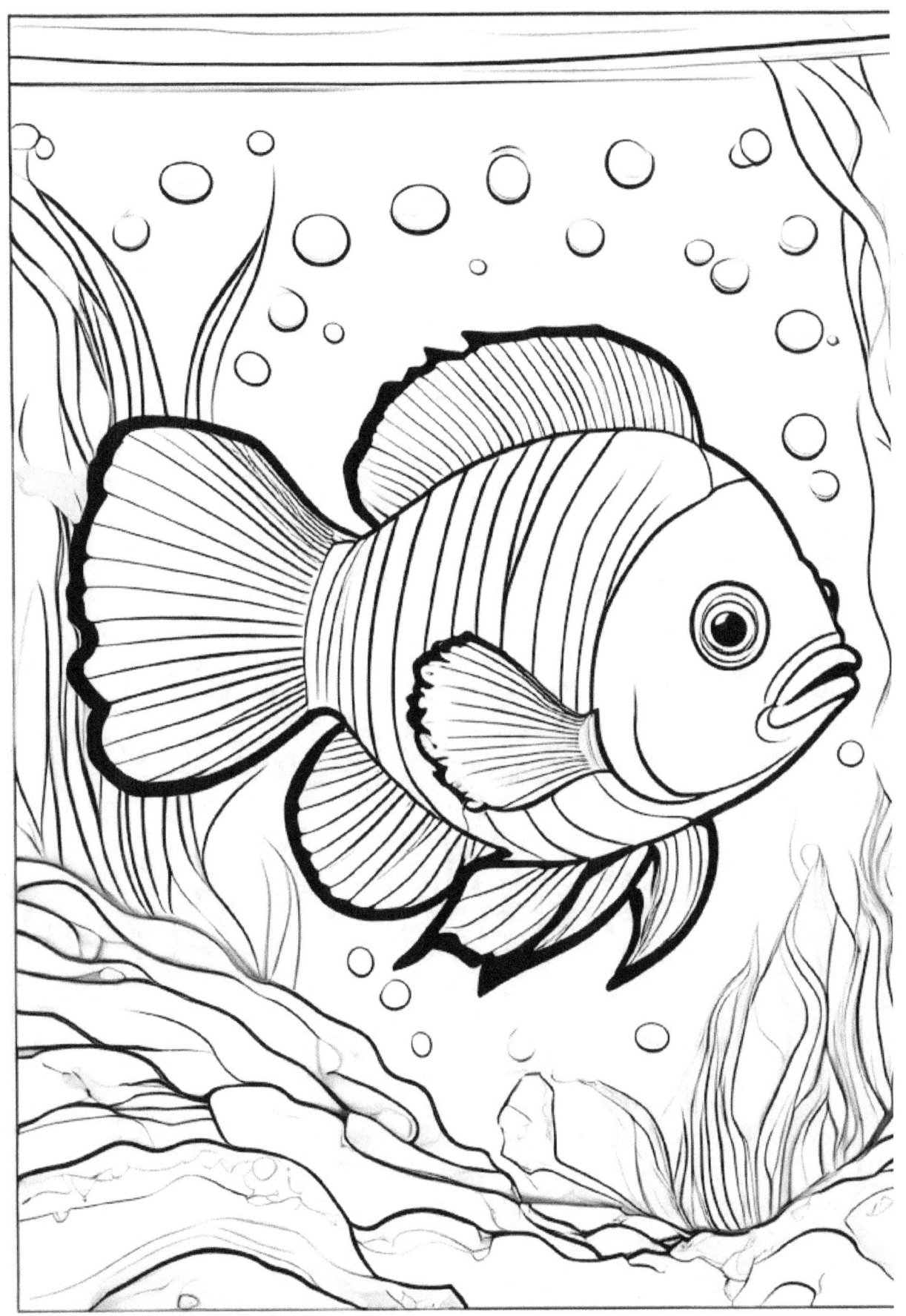

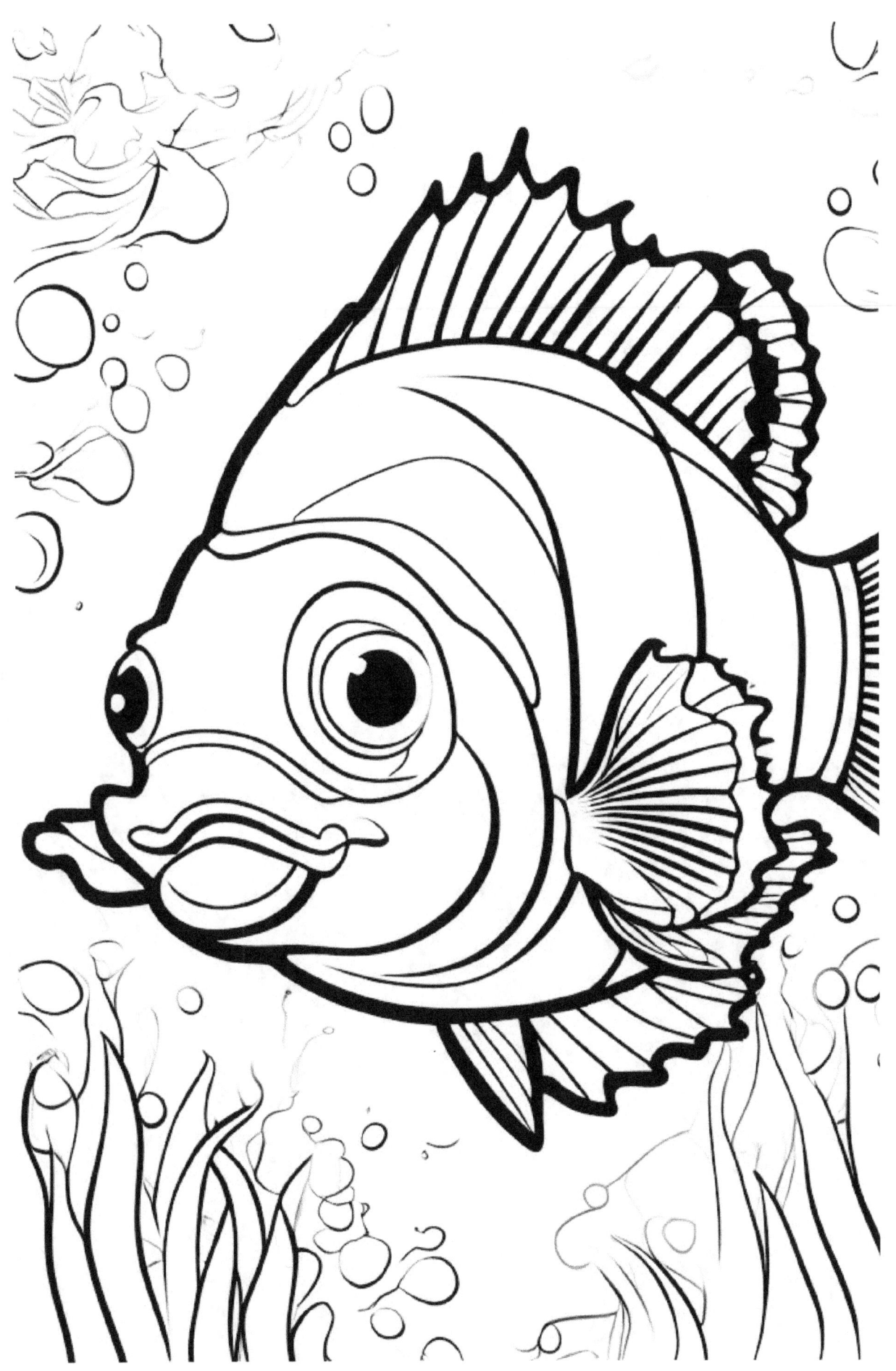

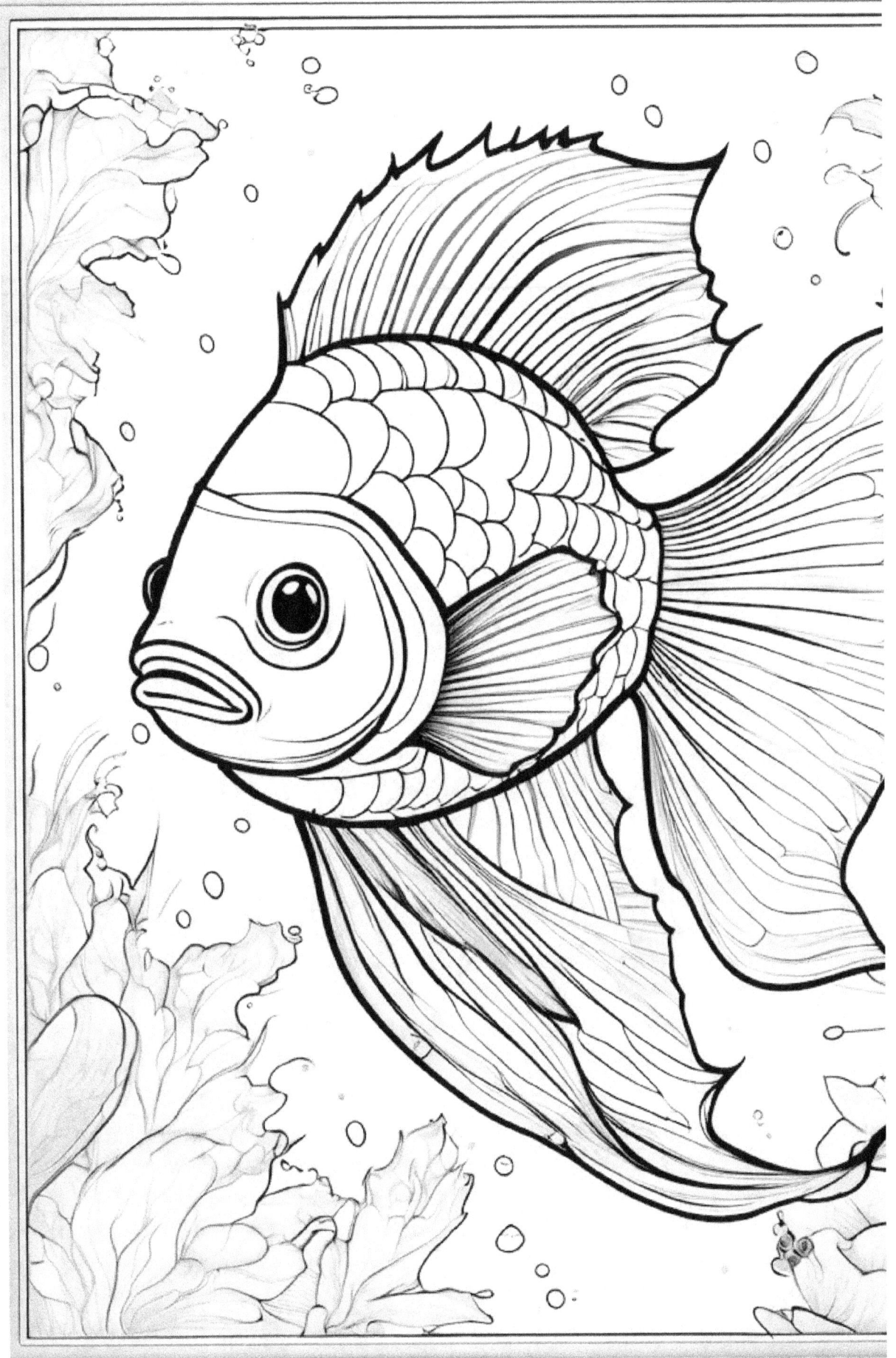

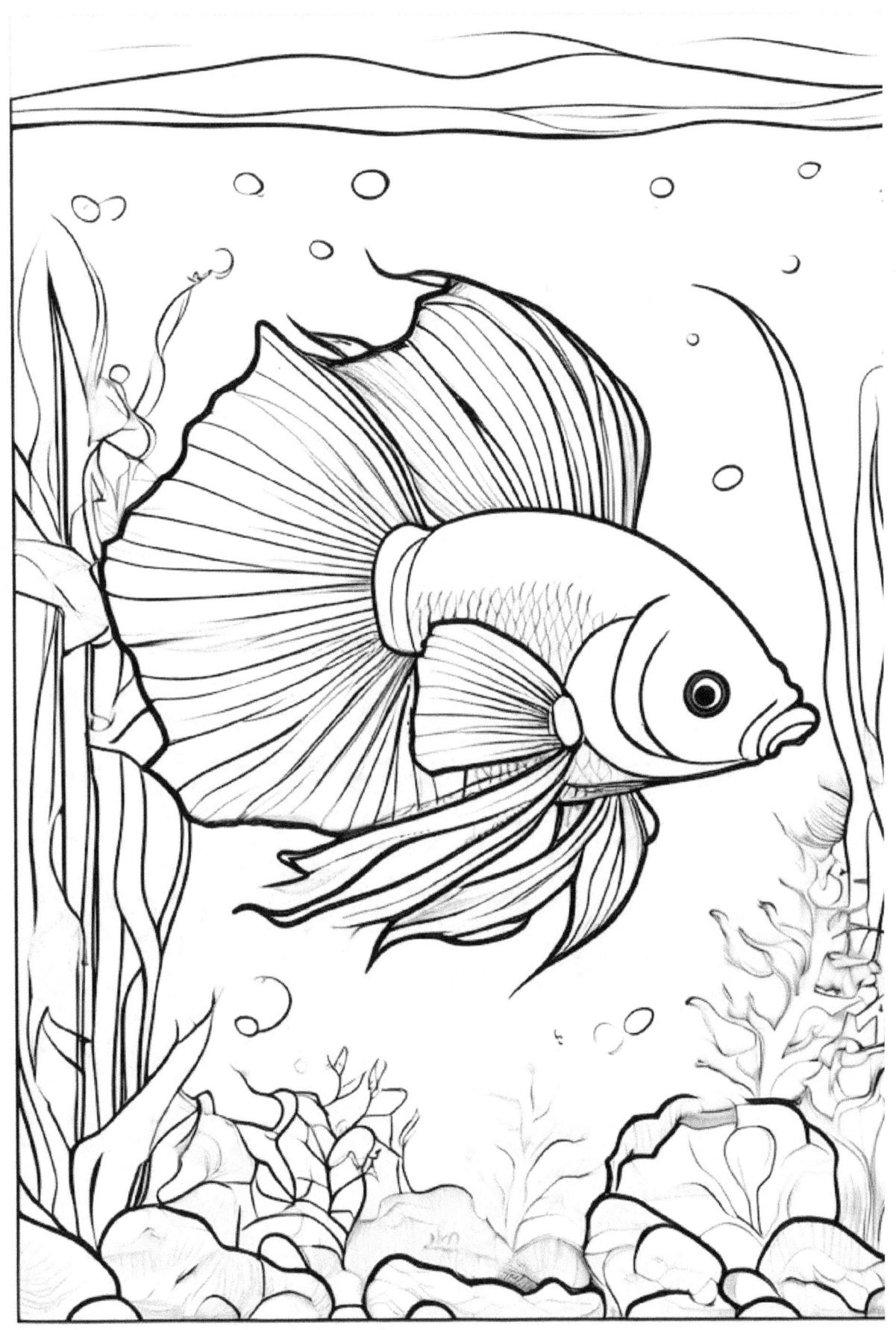

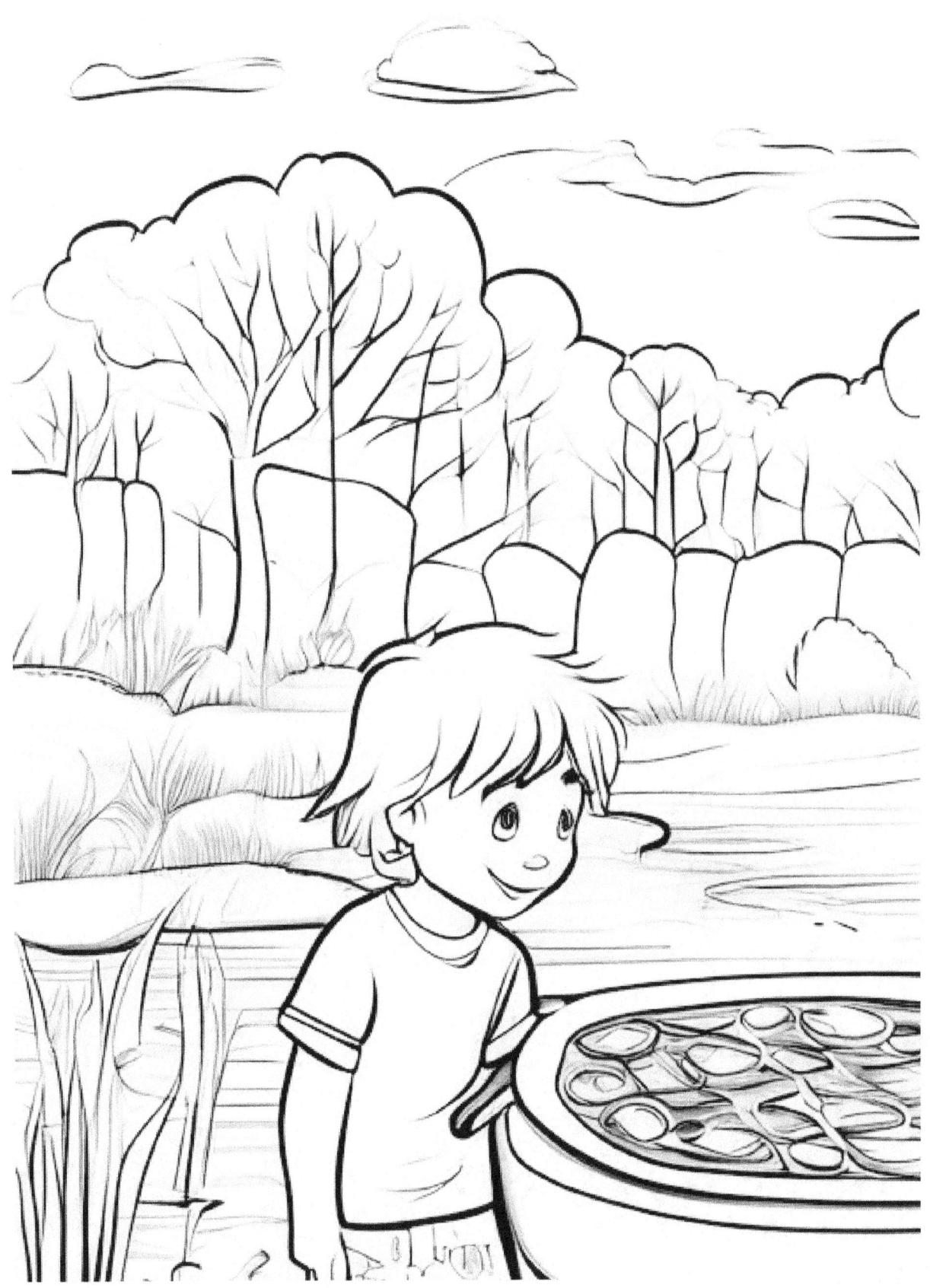